THE ORIGINAL
OLD WEST
COOKBOOK Two

Recipes in the Chuckwagon, Pioneer and Southwest Traditions

- Meats and Main Courses
- Barbeque • Chili, Soups & Stews
- Game Meats • Salads
- Fruits and Vegetables
- Breads • Desserts • Beverages
- Home Remedies and

Over 235 Recipes Inside

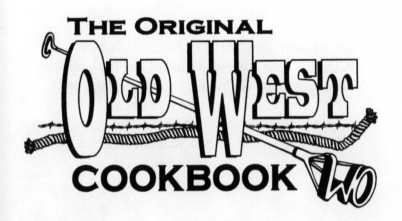

THE ORIGINAL OLD WEST COOKBOOK TWO

A Collection of Recipes
in the
Chuckwagon, Pioneer,
and Southwest Traditions

Printed in the United States of America.

ISBN: 978-1-938653-12-4

TABLE OF CONTENTS

CHAPTER 1

CHAPTER 2

CHAPTER 3

Chili, Soups and Stews

CHAPTER 4

Game Meats

CHAPTER 5

CHAPTER 6

Baked Stuffed Pumpkin
Green Chile and Potatoes
Green Chile and Squash
Herdsman's Potatoes
Okra and Tomatoes
Fire Hole Beans
Golden Baked Potatoes
Hopping John
Corn with Pinto Beans
Succotash
Tequila Lime Sweet Potatoes
Chili Squash
Baked Pumpkin
Zucchini Casserole
Spiced Red Cabbage
Roasted Onions
Eggplant Soufflé
Zucchini with Corn and Peppers
Pumpkin Butter
Beet Pickles
Green Tomato and Cheese

CHAPTER 7

Breads

Sourdough Starter
Honey-Wheat Germ Sourdough
Sourdough Raisin Bread
Spoon Bread
Sourdough Pumpernickle
Sheepherder Bread
Sourdough Camp Bread
Trapper's Sourdough Bread
Boston Brown Bread
Pioneer Bread
Sourdough Pancakes
Bolillos
Blue Corn Bread
Sour Milk Biscuits
Corn Doughgods
Moyettes
Jalapeño Spoonbread
Navajo Fry Bread
Sopaipillas
Rhubarb Bread
Tortillas

CHAPTER 8

CHAPTER 9

Beverages and Spirits

CHAPTER 10

Home Remedies and Household Hints

PHOTO CREDITS

Cover
(Los Angeles County Museum of Natural History)

Introduction
(Wisconsin State Historical Society)

Meats and Main Courses
(Colorado Historical Society)

Barbeque
(L.A. Huffman Collection)

Chilies, Soups, and Stews
(Wyoming State Museum)

Game Meats
(San Diego Historical Society)

Salads
(San Diego Historical Society)

Fruits and Vegetables
(San Diego Historical Society)

Breads
(L.A. Huffman Collection)

Desserts
(San Diego Historical Society)

Beverages and Spirits
(San Diego Historical Society)

Home Remedies and Household Hints
(Murphy Library, University of Wisconsin at La Crosse)

Back Cover
(San Diego Historical Society)

Introduction

To appreciate Western cooking, it helps to know a little of the history of the Old West, which in most cases is as vivid and spicy as the cooking. The story of course begins with the Indians. The Southwestern tribes lived in permanent villages, growing corn, beans, squash and other native crops, often with the help of irrigation. The northernmost of these tribes were the Pueblo Indians (pueblo is Spanish for village) of the upper Rio Grande in what is now New Mexico and Colorado. For a thousand years and more they had led their communal lives in almost total isolation, but it was these civilized Indians who made Southwest so different from other areas. The food of the upper Rio Grande is strongly influenced by the Indians, notably in the use of corn.

After the Indians, the next great influence on Western food were the Spanish. The Spaniards introduced cattle into Mexico and the Southwest. Wherever grass and water were to be found for their herds, Spanish cattlemen established ranches. They populated a little of Texas, and established only a few ranches in Arizona and California. The temperate, fertile valley of the upper Rio Grande, in what is now New Mexico, was just what they liked.

During the 18th Century, as the power of Spain declined, other nationalities began to exert their influence on the overextended Spanish holdings. In the mid-1700's the Russians began to move down toward California from Alaska and Anglos were advancing westward from the English colonies on the Atlantic Coast.

Even though the Spanish settlers built up enormous herds of cattle and maintained a feudal style of life, their small population increased slowly, and by the mid-1800's it was too late. Across the Rockies came the English-speaking frontiersmen, well-armed, well-organized and as tough as any men on earth. The Spanish, poorly supported by Mexico, were overwhelmed.

Yet the traditions of the Spanish and Indians remained as central elements in western food, forming the foundation of what we now call Southwest cooking. Chuckwagon cooks and others who prepared food on the trail assimilated recipes encountered along the way and made them distinctly their own. The pioneers that came from the East adopted native spices and unique foods into their traditional fare, and the true food of the Old West was born. English, German, Dutch, French... all of Europe supplied settlers to the Old West, and bits of all these cultures and their varied foods and cooking styles found their way into the spicy melting pot of Old West cooking.

Meats and
Main Courses

B eef was definitely the most popular meat in the Old West. Dating from the days of the early cattle drives, beef has been eaten in copious quantities just for its own sake.

Cowboys liked their steaks fried and done well. There's a story about a cowboy in a fine hotel dining room who ordered a steak that arrived at his table broiled to a perfect medium rare. He sent it back to the kitchen complaining, "I've seen cows git well that was hurt worse'n that."

The range cook invented what we call chicken-fried steak today. Because range cattle could be tough, the camp cook would lay a hindquarter up on the work area of the chuckwagon and slice off some medium-thick slabs of meat. Then he would pound them with a cleaver and coat them with salt, pepper, and flour. A good-sized chunk of beef suet was rendered in the Dutch oven and the cracklings skimmed out. The steaks were dropped in the sizzling fat, the oven was covered, and the steaks allowed to cook. A "sop" was made by throwing a little flour in the drippings, browning it, then adding water to make a good brown gravy. Cowboys always requested this meal and were known to quit an outfit if a reasonable number of steak dinners were not served.

Cattlemen had some interesting customs when it came to killing beef. They preferred not to eat their own cattle and would trade meat with another outfit when they could. They also could not age their beef, but killed it in the late afternoon so the meat could chill in the cool night air. When the camp moved the next day the meat was wrapped in tarps and placed under bedrolls in the wagon to protect it from the heat of the day. The meat was recooled each night and in just a few days was all eaten.

The range cooks had to do their cooking over an open fire in the most primitive of conditions. Most pioneer housewives did their cooking in open-hearth fireplaces in conditions not much better than the chuckwagon cook. The only real difference was her kitchen didn't have to move every day. The mere size and weight of cookstoves, along with the often rugged wagon trails, halted their widespread use until the end of the 1800's.

Both camp cooks and settlers made good use of the Dutch oven. The original Dutch oven was a three-legged cast-iron pot that could be placed oven the open coals in a fireplace or campfire. Meats could be fried, soups and stews could simmer, and breads and puddings could be baked in this universally used cooking utensil. The Dutch oven was quickly adapted to the woodburning stove for stovetop use. Its use is called for in many traditional recipes. You'll find that modern methods are more convenient, but Dutch oven can still be used today to capture the flavor and spirit of the Old West.

DEMI-MONDE TENDERLOIN STEAK WITH MUSHROOMS

2 tenderloin steaks
1 cup mushrooms
1 tablespoon lard or vegetable oil
1 tablespoon flour
3 tablespoons of butter or margarine
salt and pepper
1 slice toasted bread
parsley
endive

Tenderloins should come from mature beef. Dark red flesh with white fat marbling is ideal. Brighter red meat is less mature or improperly aged. Two tenderloins about 5 inches in diameter and one inch thick are just about right.

Let tenderloins come to room temperature and heat iron griddle to smoking hot. Wipe it with a clean, damp cloth before adding lard or vegetable oil and allow to heat until heat patterns form. Place tenderloins on griddle and move them to a fresh greased spot on the griddle in ten seconds. Then cover with a light tin lid.

In another small, hot frying pan melt the butter. Dredge mushrooms in flour and put into pan with butter and allow to sauté until tender. Be sure to shake the frying pan with the tenderloins from time to time. Allow them to fry until almost the proper point on the first side, then turn over for a quick braising. Place them on a large platter. Sprinkle ground pepper on the griddle and add a little water. Let cook briefly, stir with a spatula and dribble over meat. Salt and pepper lightly.

Add a little butter to the griddle, fry a slice of lightly toasted bread on one side and place around platter. Garnish with parsley and endive. Serve with commercial steak sauce or make your own (recipe follows).

OLD WEST STEAK SAUCE

4-pound soupbone
6 whole cloves
water
bay leaf
1 teaspoon of salt
1 bunch green onions
1 tablespoon of peppercorns
1/3 cup of butter or margarine
flour as needed
1/3 cup marrow

Choose a soupbone that has some good red meat. In a pot, half cover with cold water and add salt, peppercorns, bay leaf, and cloves. Slowly bring to a boil and let simmer for about 5 hours. Remove the bone, strain, and let stand until cold. Remove grease from the top. Add finely chopped green onions, butter, and chopped marrow. Boil until the amount is reduced to 4 cups. Strain again. Make a thin paste of flour and cold water and add slowly while stirring constantly. Add just enough to slightly thicken the sauce. Store in the refrigerator and serve warm as needed.

BAKED RIVER FISH

1 whole fish, 4 to 8 pounds
1 onion
cracker crumbs
1 carrot
1/4 pound salt pork
1 teaspoon vinegar
1 cup canned milk
1 tablespoon sugar
1 cup water
salt and pepper
capers, sweet pickles optional

Choose a channel cat, small sturgeon, a carp from good water, or a trout such as Loch Laven or a large river rainbow. Remove head and tail. Skin fish or scale it, depending on the species. Even trout which are not customarily scaled often require a little work when they're in the large size.

Heat a roaster in a hot oven, about 400 degrees, and fry salt pork slices until crisp. Remove the pork, dredge the fish inside and out in cracker crumbs, and start it sizzling in the grease. Add the canned milk, water, sliced onion, and quartered carrot. Cover, turn down the heat, and cook until the fish, onion, and carrot are well-done. Salt and pepper to taste. Remove the fish carefully to prevent it from breaking.

Garnish with the carrots, onion, and crisp salt pork. To milk thickened by cracker crumbs that remains in the pan, add vinegar and sugar. You may add more if taste requires. Capers will lend a spicy flavor. Some cooks delete sugar, vinegar, and capers and add chopped sweet pickles in their place. Blend until smooth and serve as a sauce.

FANCY SIX-SHOOTER STEAK

If you don't have a six shooter in your kitchen you can make this authentic recipe using modern utensils.

2 thick, full-cut round steaks
1 cup flour
1 teaspoon peppercorns
3 tablespoons Worcestershire sauce
1 cup lard or vegetable oil
salt

Pulverize the peppercorns by crushing (don't grind) them on a slab of hardwood or heavy cutting board. Brush them into the cup of flour. Cut round steaks into desired size. Using a meat mallet, pound them while sprinkling lightly with flour and pepper. Don't hammer just pound lightly. Don't work the meat too thin. Steaks are best when reduced to about two-thirds of their original thickness.

When each is finished, sprinkle it with Worcestershire sauce. Stack the steaks one on the other and allow them to cure for 1/2 hour. Melt lard or vegetable oil in a covered skillet or Dutch oven and fry until browned while still raw in the middle. Salt, cover tightly, and set off the heat. By the time the skillet is cool, the steaks will be done all the way through and a gravy will be formed which delicately coats each of them.

Santa Fe Bob sez:

Fresh vegetables were hard to come by out on the range. Big cattle ranchers sometimes didn't grow as much as one potato. All supplies had to be hauled from miles away.

Homesteaders almost always had vegetables to trade for a piece of beef, and cooks drove their wagons many miles off course to get them.

Camp cooks knew that tough meat could be tenderized by taking a thick cut and pounding it. They used a dull butcher knife, a chain flail or even the side of a dish. But the favored utensil among old-time cooks was the six-shooter. The standard Peacemaker colt, single action .45 caliber with a 7-1/2" barrel had good weight and balance. The barrel fit the hand, and the butt was perfectly shaped to tenderize the meat without punching holes through it. The six shooter was also used to pulverize peppercorns and other various spices.

GREEN CHICKEN ENCHILADAS

1/3 cup half & half
6 ounces cream cheese, softened
2 cups shredded cooked chicken breasts
3/4 cup finely chopped onion
1/2 teaspoon salt
Tomatillo Sauce (see recipe below)
3/4 cup each shredded Jack and Cheddar cheese
12 corn tortillas
vegetable oil
lettuce, ripe olives, tomatoes and sour cream for garnish

Beat together half & half and cream cheese until smooth and fluffy. Add chicken, onion and salt and blend well. Soften tortillas in hot oil, then dip into sauce for 30 seconds. Spoon a thin layer of Tomatillo Sauce into a baking dish then place a coated tortilla in the dish. Place about 1/4 cup of chicken mixture down the center of each.. Roll tortillas leaving flap side down. Pour a little sauce on top. Heat in 350°F oven covered with foil about 20 minutes. Remove, sprinkle cheese on top and cook uncovered for 5 more minutes. Serve with garnish and remaining sauce. Serves 4 to 6.

TOMATILLO SAUCE
2 dozen tomatillos, husked
4 to 6 serrano peppers, stemmed, seeded and minced
3 cups chicken broth
2 tablespoons cornstarch
1 teaspoon salt
2 tablespoons chopped fresh cilantro

Boil tomatoes and peppers in chicken broth about 7 minutes. Dissolve cornstarch in a small amount of cold water and add to boiling mixture along with salt and cilantro. Boil for another 5 minutes, allow to cool slightly and purée until smooth.

CHILE SCAMPI

3/4 cup extra virgin olive oil
12 large garlic cloves, coarsely chopped
1 1/2 tablespoons crushed dried red chile
3 pounds large fresh shrimp, peeled,
de-veined and well washed
1 1/2 tablespoons fresh lime juice

In a large heavy frying pan, heat the olive oil over medium-high heat. Add the garlic, and as it starts to brown, add the dried chile and the shrimp at the same time, slightly lowering the heat. Quickly cook and stir.

Add the freshly squeezed lime juice, evenly distributing it over the shrimp as they are cooking. Saute only until done, about 5 minutes. Serve hot on a heated platter arranged around the edge of Polka Dot Rice (recipe follows). Serves 12.

POLKA DOT RICE

4 tablespoons sweet butter
1 cup diced green bell pepper
1 cup diced red bell pepper
1 cup finely chopped Spanish onion
4 garlic cloves, minced
2 cups basmati rice
1/2 teaspoon ground oregano
1 teaspoon ground cumin
6 cups rich chicken stock
2 tablespoons minced fresh parsley

Melt butter in a large heavy skillet, then add the peppers, onion, garlic, rice, oregano, and cumin. Saute until the rice looks well glazed and is slightly golden.

Add the chicken stock and bring to a boil. Cover and simmer for 15 minutes. Remove lid, stir, and set lid ajar to allow to fluff for 5 minutes. Garnish with parsley.

STUFFED CHINESE PORK ROAST

When the Union Pacific and Central Pacific Railroads joined together at Promontory Point, Utah, the Chinese laborers who had been brought in by the thousands to work in the construction found themselves cut loose in the strange environment of the Old West. Many of them went into mining, but a great number of them went into business and in particular the restaurant business. Since the average western diet favored roasts, chops and stews, the Chinese used these ingredients in their own unique fashion.

2 pork shoulders
1 apple
3/4 teaspoon salt
1 stalk celery
1 pound dried fruit (peaches, pears, apricots, apples)
1 powdered sage leaf
1 quart water
1/4 teaspoon thyme
1 teaspoon ginger
1/2 teaspoon salt
2 slices dry bread
cornstarch
soy sauce
1 onion, optional

Simmer fruits with double their weight of water along with ginger. Bone the two pork shoulders and soak them in the warm liquor from the dried fruit for 1/2 hour. Cut bread into bite-sized pieces and mix in a bowl with stuffing ingredients. Add enough water to just soak the bread. Lay stuffing on one opened shoulder and place the other over it. Skewer together, but do not roll. Steam for 1/2 hour in a hot oven then brown on higher heat. Don't overcook. Thicken drippings with cornstarch, water and a little soy sauce for gravy.

MINTED TROUT

1 fresh trout
1/2 cup olive or vegetable oil
mint, wild or garden variety
2 strips of bacon

Mix mint with salt and olive or vegetable oil and mash together to bring out the flavor of the mint. Fill the cavity of trout with mint leaves. Wrap the trout with mint leaves and bind with one or two strips of bacon. Secure the bacon with a round toothpick. Broil until the bacon is cooked. To serve, remove the mint from the trout. The bacon and mint gives the trout a wonderful, mystical herb flavor.

HANGTOWN FRY

According to Goldrush legend, a crusty miner found his way into the town of Hangtown (now called Placerville, CA) and demanded the most expensive meal they had. Since eggs and oysters were the costliest items on the menu, this is what he got.

1 dozen small, Pacific coast oysters
1/2 cup flour, seasoned with salt and black pepper
1 cup of cracker crumbs
1/2 cup butter or margarine
9 eggs
red and green pepper pieces for garnish

Dry oysters on a paper towel. Dip in flour, then into one beaten egg. Then dip into cracker crumbs. Fry in butter until browned. Beat 8 eggs and add to oysters. Cook slowly until firm. Garnish with pepper pieces.

Santa Fe Bob Sez:

Oysters were a favorite food of the Old West. The first canneries were built near oyster ports, and it was their output that the inland pioneers knew. In those days shellfish were scraped up from the sea bottoms of eastern and Gulf coastal waters where Nature had put them. But oyster farming became necessary to meet the demand. .

Oysters were transported by wagon freight and were kept cold with ice from the local ice houses on the route. The oysters were fed a mixture of salt water and corn meal poured down through the barrels. They stayed fat and healthy on their journey. A six to eight-inch oyster was common place.

Oysters were a thrilling and exotic fare for people of the Old West whose diet consisted largely of pork fat, flour, and beans. Champagne and cold oysters were a favorite in Santa Fe, NM and Lincoln was famous in Illinois for his oyster roasts.. Pickled oysters were a favorite of the nineteenth-century, in fact, President U.S. Grant was known to have liked them better than almost any other food.

~~+~+~+~+~+~+~+~+~+~+~+~+~+~+~+~+~+~

PICKLED OYSTERS

100 large oysters
(ask for "counts" rather than the smaller "standards")
1 tablespoon salt
1 pint cider vinegar
2 sticks cinnamon
1 teaspoon allspice
1/2 teaspoon cloves
1 teaspoon peppercorns
1 hot red pepper, fresh or dried

Put the large oysters and their liquid into a pot, with enough water to just cover, and cook until they barely begin to boil. Add a little salt. Skim off the scum on top; then remove the oysters, and set them aside to cool. Add vinegar to the juice, the pepper without seeds, and the other spices. Heat this to a boil to release the flavor of the spices. Put the oysters in jars and pour the hot pickling juice over them. Cool and keep in the refrigerator. They will be ready to eat within two days and are delicious!

OYSTER CATSUP

1 pint oysters with juice
1 cup sherry wine
1 tablespoon salt
1 teaspoon cayenne pepper
1 teaspoon mace

Scald oysters in their juice with wine. Strain the oysters, finely chop, and add salt, cayenne pepper and mace. Add to liquid in which the oysters were cooked and boil for five minutes. Skim well and run through a sieve. When cold, bottle and seal.

CHILIES RELLENOS

*12 large, mild green chilies with stems on
(if fresh ones are not available, buy three 4-ounce cans)
8 ounces Monterey Jack cheese,
cut into long narrow strips
Batter (recipe follows)
vegetable oil or lard*

First parch the chilies using this method. Rinse, drain and pierce each one close to the stem. If chili is large, piece twice, once on each side. Place chilies on a cookie sheet, cover with foil and broil. Rotate chilies as they turn amber so skin blisters uniformly. Remove chilies and place in a bowl and cover with a cold, damp towel for 10 minutes. This steams the chilies to make peeling easier. Peel the chilies starting at the stem end and peeling downward. Leave the stems on.

Open a small slit below the stem and remove seeds if desired. Insert strips of cheese into the chilies, using care not to split them. Place on paper towels to drain.

Heat oil in a large skillet. Dip each cheese-stuffed chile into the batter and fry until golden. If you deep-fry the chilies they look rounder and fluffier. Drain on absorbent paper towels and serve immediately. Top with green chile and serve with refried beans.

BATTER
*5 egg yolks
2 tablespoons of flour
1/4 teaspoon salt
1/4 teaspoon baking powder
5 egg whites*

Mix together egg yolks, flour, salt and baking powder. Set aside. Beat egg whites until stiff peaks form. Just before ready to use fold egg yolk mixture into egg whites.

NEW MEXICAN FLANK STEAK

3 chorizo sausages (about 3/4 lb. total),
casings removed
1-1/2 cups unseasoned croutons
1/2 cup each chopped green onions(including tops)
and parsley
2 lightly beaten eggs
1-l/2 to 2 pounds flank steak
3 tablespoons salad oil
1 jar (12 oz.) green chile salsa

Crumble sausage into a wide frying pan. Cook over medium heat, stirring, until meat is browned. Drain off fat and remove from heat. Stir in croutons, onions, parsley, and eggs.

Butterfly steak by slicing in half horizontally almost all the way through. Spread open and pound to 1/2 inch thickness. Spoon sausage mixture over half the steak. Fold ends in, roll to enclose, and tie securely with string.

Heat oil in frying pan over medium-high heat; add meat and brown evenly on all sides. Transfer to an ungreased 2-quart baking dish and pour salsa over all.

Cover and bake in a 375° oven until meat is tender when pierced (about 1-3/4 hours). Remove string. Skim and discard fat. Bake some carrots and onions at the same time and serve all together with sauce spooned on top. Makes about 6 servings.

BEEF AND PORK PICADO

*2 pounds each lean boneless beef chuck
and boneless pork butt or shoulder
2 medium-size onions, cut into wedges
2 medium-size green bell peppers,
seeded and cut into large chunks
2 cups regular-strength beef broth
4 medium-size tomatoes, cut into wedges
4 garlic cloves, minced or pressed
1 fresh or pickled jalapeño chile, including seeds, minced
1/4 teaspoon pepper
salt*

Cut beef and pork, including any fat, into 1-1/2 inch cubes and place in a 5- to 6-quart pan. Cover and cook over medium-high heat to draw out juices (about 10 minutes). Uncover and cook over high heat until liquid evaporates; stir occasionally. Add onions and bell peppers; cook, stirring frequently, until meat is evenly browned. Add broth, tomatoes, garlic, chile, and pepper. Stir to free browned bits from bottom of pan.

Reduce heat, cover, and simmer until meat is tender enough to shred easily with a fork (about 2-1/2 hours).

Uncover and boil over medium-high heat until juices are reduced to just below top of meat and are slightly thickened, stirring more frequently as mixture thickens. Season to taste with salt. Makes about 8 servings.

RED RIVER CHICKEN

1 young frying chicken (about 2 1/2 pounds)
2 tablespoons sweet butter
3 zucchini squash
4 ears fresh corn kernels cut off the cob
OR 2-1/2 cups defrosted, frozen corn
2 large, fresh red ripe tomatoes (1 pound each)
2 small white or yellow Spanish onions
3 garlic cloves, minced
1 chopped jalapeño
1/2 teaspoon cumin

Melt the butter over medium heat in a large heavy skillet, Dutch oven, or even a deep cast-iron pot, as long as it has a tight-fitting cover. Add the chicken, skin side down, and turn frequently to brown evenly.

Cut zucchini into bite-sized slices on the bias. Parch and peel the tomatoes, then cut into wedges. Cut onions into thin rounds. When the chicken is browned, add the vegetables in layers—zucchini, corn, tomatoes, and onions. Sprinkle the garlic, jalapeño, and cumin over the top, cover, and steam, reducing heat to just maintain steaming. Check after 30 minutes to be certain all is cooking properly. Then continue to cook for about 30 minutes longer, or until vegetables are done. To serve, place on a platter with the chicken encircled with the vegetables. For added zip serve with salsa (recipe follows).

CHICKEN SALSA

1 jalapeno, about 3 inches long finely chopped
1 small chopped, ripe tomato
1/4 cup chopped red Spanish onion

Combine and serve in a small bowl with the chicken.

TAMALES

Tamales are a lot of work to make, but as an authentic Southwestern recipe there is no equal. Tamales can be frozen for a year without losing any flavor, so you can make a large batch with a variety of fillings. Be sure to remove the husk before saucing and eating.

BEEF FILLING
3 pounds cubed round steak
1/4 cup bacon drippings, lard or shortening
1/4 cup flour
1/2 cup ground mild chili
1 quart beef stock
2 teaspoons salt
1/2 teaspoon oregano
3 minced garlic cloves

Simmer beef in water to cover for 1 hour, or until very tender. Remove from heat and cool. Cut into very tiny cubes by hand to give the best texture and appearance.

Melt drippings or lard in a large, heavy pan. Add beef cubes and stir in the flour. Mix well and when lightly golden, remove from heat.

Stir in ground chili and when well combined, add half the beef stock. Cook and stir until well mixed, then add salt, oregano, and garlic. Continue to add beef stock a little at a time. Cook for about 30 minutes more, or until the filling is very thick and smooth.

Proceed with filling and rolling as described in the Tamale Masa recipe that follows. Makes 10 to 12 dozen tamales.

VARIATION: A great chicken filling can be made with 6 cups of cooked, boned and shredded chicken. Combine chicken with 1 pint of sour cream and 4 cups of coarsely grated Monterey Jack cheese and salt to taste. Fill and roll as in Tamale Masa recipe adding a strip or two of parched peeled and seeded fresh green chili down the center of each. **For a sweet tamale, see DESSERTS.**

TAMALE MASA

7 cups warm water
12 cups masa harina
3 cups shortening or lard
1-1/2 tablespoons salt
10 to 12 dozen dried corn husks cleaned and trimmed

Begin by soaking the corn husks in hot water (about 30 minutes). Add 7 cups warm water to the masa and stir to combine well, then allow to set for 15 or more minutes. The mixture should be the texture of a firm pudding—if too soft, add more masa; if hard and dry, add more warm water.

With an electric mixer on high, whip the shortening until very fluffy. Sprinkle in the salt, then add the masa a little at a time with the mixer running on low speed. When all has been well mixed, you are ready to roll tamales.

Using a rubber scraper, place 2 or more tablespoons of the masa mixture in a 3 x 4-inch rectangle of corn husk, centered lengthwise on each. The masa should be about 1/4 inch thick. Allow at least a 1-1/2 inch margin on the top and bottom. Place a thin strip of your choice of tamale filling down the very center. Hold the sides of the husks up, join them together, and roll to enclose the filling. Fold up the bottom, broader end, and tie using a strip of corn husk, fastening it with a bow. Then either crimp the tops together or fold down and tie with a strip of corn husk.

When you're ready to cook, place the tamales upright in a steaming basket, and steam tightly covered, for about 45 minutes, or until the masa is firm. Check while steaming to be sure there is at least an inch of water at all times to generate adequate steam.

SALSAS

Fresh table sauces, or salsas, have a variety of uses and can be used in combination with many dishes. Enjoy as a dipping sauce for warm tostadas, spoon over hamburgers, or serve as an addition to main courses or side dishes. Do try to make them just an hour or less before serving, as they are best when served very fresh.

SALSA FRESCA

*1 cup finely diced red, ripe tomato,
excess juice and seeds removed
1 cup finely diced Spanish onion,
preferably red and white mixed
1 cup finely diced green chilies,
parched, peeled, and de-seeded
2 garlic cloves, finely minced
1-1/2 teaspoons salt*

Combine all the ingredients in an earthenware or porcelain bowl. Stir gently and set aside for at least 30 minutes before serving. Spoon on to cheese appetizers, chili, tamales, eggs, meat fish or poultry. Makes 3 cups.

COLD SALSA VERDE

*1/2 cup coarsely chopped Spanish onions
2 tablespoons fresh cilantro
1 fresh or pickled jalapeño pepper, or to taste
1/2 teaspoon of salt
1 can (10 ounces) undrained tomatillos*

Place all ingredients in a blender or food processor. Puree them, then adjust seasonings for desired hotness. This traditional green sauce is excellent over chicken, seafood, or pork dishes and is also used a a table relish.

JALAPEÑO MAYONNAISE

In a blender or food processor, combine 3 or 4 fresh jalapeño or other small hot chilies, stemmed, seeded, and minced; 1 clove garlic, minced or pressed; 1 large egg yolk; 2 tablespoons lime juice; and 1/2 teaspoon salt. Blend until smoothly pureed. Continue to blend and slowly add 3/4 cup salad oil, a drop at a time first, then in a slow stream, until all oil is added and mixture is very thick. Cover and refrigerate for at least 1 hour or up to 3 days before serving. Makes a great sauce for grilled fish, chicken or a spread for sandwiches. Makes about 1 cup.

CHILE HOLLANDAISE

Place 1 large (5 to 6-inch) dried red New Mexico or California chile in a 9-inch square baking pan. Bake in a 300° oven until chile smells toasted (about 4 minutes). Let cool slightly. Discard stem and seeds. Crumble chile into small pieces.

In a blender, combine chile pieces, 1 tablespoon hot water, 1/2 teaspoon ground cumin, 2 teaspoons lemon juice, and 1 egg yolk. Pureé until smooth. With blender on high speed, slowly add 1/2 cup (1/4 pound) melted butter or margarine in a slow, steady stream, until well blended. Use hot or at room temperature for Eggs Benedict or fish dishes. Makes 3/4 cup.

CODFISH BALLS

Salt cod was a staple food in the Old West. In the days before flash-freezing, ocean fish headed for inland markets had to be salted, smoked, or canned (sometimes all three). Cod taken from the Atlantic by New England fishermen were put in brine, then drained and packed in long flat wooden boxes for shipment.

1/2 pound moist salt cod
1 teaspoon of vinegar
1 pound of potatoes
2 eggs
pepper
lard or vegetable oil

Place cod in bowl with tap water, add vinegar, cover and let soak at room temperature overnight.

Next morning, wash and peel the potatoes and simmer in water until they break easily with a fork, about 20 to 25 minutes. While potatoes cook, drain the cod and flake it into a small saucepan. Be sure to remove any tough skin, then pull flesh apart in small pieces. Cover cod with water and simmer 15 minutes. Drain well and cool.

Break the eggs into a bowl and beat them well with a fork. Drain cooked potatoes and mash with slotted spoon until smooth and cool. Put potatoes and cod into bowl, mix well with eggs and pepper.

Heat lard or vegetable oil in it until it is hot enough to brown a 1/2-inch cube of sliced bread in a minute (325°F). Drop the codfish mixture in the hot fat by rounded teaspoonfuls, four or five at a time. The balls should brown in 1 to 2 minutes. Remove them when brown to a warm plate with paper towel to drain. Repeat with remaining mixture. Makes 6 servings, 5 codfish balls each.

HOMEMADE COUNTRY SAUSAGE

The texture and flavor you will find in this hand-chopped sausage is distinctly different from commercial products, even though the ingredients are the same. To make country sausage without butchering, ask a butcher for quantities of lean and fat pork, or buy a loin or shoulder of four pounds or more and cut it apart yourself.

> *pork, 2 pounds of lean and 1 pound fat*
> *1 tablespoon salt*
> *1 teaspoon pepper*
> *1 tablespoon crumbled, dried sage*

Separate the lean and fat pork, using boning knife. With a very sharp chef's knife, cut both into 1-inch cubes. Start to mince the cubes a few at a time. Put chopped fat in smaller bowl and chopped lean in larger one. Keep the bowl you're not working on and unchopped cubes covered in refrigerator.

In the large bowl combine choppings, adding one part fat for every two parts of lean. Add seasoning. With hands that have been washed with unscented soap blend the sausage and shape it in individual patties to freeze or to fry immediately.

Brown sausage cakes in skillet for 4 to 6 minutes over medium-high heat. Turn and brown the other side. Lower the heat, cover the pan, and cook the cakes throughly for 15 to 20 minutes more. Pork should always be well cooked. Remove cakes to a warm platter and make gravy.

GRAVY: Beat 2 tablespoons flour into 1 cup milk. Pour into the skillet over low heat and stir until it is thick and bubbly and the pan is scraped clean. Taste and correct seasoning. Serve the gravy separately. Although this lean sausage is well suited to modern tastes, the fat gravy may not be.

POT ROAST AND
SOUR CREAM GRAVY

4 pound beef pot roast
3 tablespoons vegetable oil
1 beef bouillon cube
1 cup boiling water
2 tablespoons ketchup
2 tablespoons Worcestershire sauce
1/4 cup onions, minced
1/2 clove garlic. minced
2 teaspoons salt
1 teaspoon celery seed
1/8 teaspoon black pepper
1/2 cup sliced fresh mushrooms
4 tablespoons flour
1 cup sour cream

Brown pot roast in oil in a Dutch oven. Pour off drippings. Dissolve bouillon cube in the cup boiling water and add to roast. Add ketchup, Worcestershire sauce, onion, garlic, salt, celery seed and pepper. Cover kettle and cook over low heat 2-1/2 to 3 hours, or until meat is tender.

Remove meat from kettle. Blend flour with 1/2 cup cold water and stir into remaining beef liquid to make gravy. Add mushrooms. Remove kettle from fire and stir in sour cream. Serve slices of pot roast with gravy.

STEWED CHICKEN AND DUMPLINGS

4 to 6-pound stewing hen
4 cups water
2 stalks celery, chopped
1 cup flour
2 teaspoons baking powder
1/2 teaspoon salt
1 carrot, chopped
1 medium onion, chopped
2 teaspoons salt
3 peppercorns

DUMPLINGS

2/3 cup milk
1 tablespoon melted butter or margarine
1 tablespoon chopped parsley

Clean chicken and cut into pieces. Place in a kettle with water, celery, carrot, onion, salt and peppercorns. Bring to a boil, then reduce heat and simmer 15-20 minutes and remove surface froth or scum.

Let chicken simmer 2 hours or until meat is tender. If water boils away, add more.

Combine dumpling ingredients until just moistened and drop by spoonfuls into the slowly boiling chicken broth. Cover kettle and let dumplings cook 12-15 minutes. Place chicken pieces on a serving plate or platter and arrange dumplings around them.

STEAK AND ONION PIE

2 medium onions, sliced
1/4 cup shortening
1 pound round steak
1/4 cup flour
2 teaspoons salt
1/8 teaspoon pepper
1/2 teaspoon paprika
dash ginger
dash allspice
2-1/2 cups boiling water
3 medium potatoes, diced
1 unbaked pastry top crust

Cook onions slowly in melted shortening until yellow. Remove onions and set aside. Slice meat into one-inch cubes and toss in a mixture of flour, seasonings and spices. Brown meat cubes in the hot melted shortening.

Add boiling water. Cover skillet and cook over low heat approximately one hour. Add potatoes and cook 15 minutes more. Arrange onions over top of mixture. Pour into a greased 8-inch casserole dish. Fit pastry crust over top. Slit top with knife and seal edges of crust. Bake in 450° F. oven 25 minutes.

OLD FASHIONED MEAT LOAF

1 pound ground sirloin
1/4 pound pork sausage
1 egg, beaten
1 tablespoon butter or margarine, melted
3 slices bread, crumbled
1 onion, finely chopped
1 teaspoon salt
1/8 teaspoon black pepper
1-1/4 teaspoons ground sage
1 beef bouillon cube
1/2 cup boiling water
4 strips bacon
4 tablespoons chili sauce

Combine all ingredients except last four in a large mixing bowl. Dissolve bouillon in the boiling water and add to mixture. Shape into a loaf and place in greased baking pan. Top with bacon strips. Bake in moderate oven (350° F.). After meat has baked approximately 25 minutes, remove from oven and spoon chili sauce on top of loaf. Return to oven for another 35-40 minutes.

DUTCH OVEN INSTRUCTIONS: If baking in your Dutch oven on the stovetop, preheat oven or kettle to moderate (350° F.) and place rack or trivet on bottom of oven. Place meat loaf pan on rack. Cover Dutch oven tightly with lid and bake 15-20 minutes. Open lid and spoon chili sauce on top. Then vent lid on both sides and bake 35-40 minutes more.

FARMER'S ROASTED PIG

Since the days of the Old West ovens have gotten smaller and pigs, on average, have gotten larger. This means
you are not likely to find a pig you can stretch out straight
and roast slowly overnight. A commercially raised suckling pig, 12 to 25 pounds, must be doubled over to fit an
18-inch oven and turned during roasting, so you can't
sleep while it cooks or serve it in the traditional pose,
prone on a platter with an apple in its mouth. However, it
is still worth doing.

Pork should always be well done. This is easy to do
with the fast-cooking, well-lubricated flesh of a young
porker. At moderate temperature, 350°F., an 18-pound
suckling pig, stuffed, will be done in four hours. It will
feed up to fourteen people. Handling it in the kitchen will
take two pairs of hands.

1 dressed suckling pig, 15 to 20 pounds
8 to 10 cups stale white bread crumbs
1 pound yellow onions,
5 tablespoons butter or margarine
2 to 3 tablespoons crumbled dried sage
2 eggs
1 cup cider
1/2 cup chopped, fresh parsley,
ground nutmeg and mace, generous pinches
2 tablespoons unbleached flour
small red apple
parsley, celery leaves, or evergreen boughs for garnish

Take the largest roaster your oven will hold and ask the
butcher to lace the snout and feet with string so the pig
can be tied up to fit the pan. The pig should have clean
ears, be free of hair, and be accompanied by haslets or
organs—liver, heart, and lungs. Rinse the pig inside and
out with cold water and pat dry. Keep it cold while

preparing broth and stuffing.

To make gravy broth, simmer haslets in 2 cups of water in saucepan. After about 20 minutes, remove the liver and chop it fine to add to the stuffing.

To prepare stuffing, put dry bread crumbs or slices in a dishtowel and pound them into fine crumbs with a mallet or rolling pin. Put coarsely chopped onions into a skillet and fry until limp in 3 tablespoons of the butter. Combine crumbs, onions, and sage in large bowl.

In small bowl beat eggs and stir in cider. Add chopped parsley, nutmeg, and mace, and blend into crumb mixture. Stir in chopped liver. Preheat oven to 350°F.

Spoon the stuffing loosely into the pig's cavity and close the opening with skewers and lacing. Draw the head and back feet together with butcher's string and tie it. Place the pig in the roaster, and rub all skin surfaces generously with remaining butter. With a sharp knife slash the back skin in several places to permit fat to escape. Use wood block or small can to prop mouth open during roasting. Add 1 cup of boiling water to pan and place pig and pan in preheated oven.

Baste pig with pan juices after an hour. In another 30 minutes check for browning. When top side is thoroughly browned, turn pig over (a two-person job) and continue roasting. The pig is done when fully browned and when skin begins to shrink and break.

While the pig is roasting, chill the haslet broth and remove fat from the surface. Blend flour into the broth.

At serving time remove pig to large platter or board and cut away string. If suitable for display, replace mouth prop with the apple. Garnish platter with greens.

Skim pan gravy of excess fat and stir in floured broth. Heat and stir until gravy is thick and smooth. Season to taste and transfer to gravy bowl.

At the table, start carving by cutting off the pig's head. Next run the knife down the spine and lay the body open in two halves. Then cut into serving pieces.

Barbeque

The Spanish word barbacoa is the foundation of the word barbeque. The Spanish word was derived from an Indian word for a framework of green wood on which meat or fish could be broiled. The most ancient method of barbecuing, which under various names was used by Indians from New England to Chile, was to cook the meat over hot coals or stones set in a hole in the ground. It is still practiced by traditionalists who are willing to go to a lot of trouble, and it produces marvelous results.

Texans are known for the effort they put into barbeque. For one traditional version, the chef starts by digging a hole in the ground about three feet deep and two feet wide. If the soil is hard and clay-like, the hole should have a narrow mouth and a side vent leading to the surface from two thirds of the way down. This vent supplies air and speeds the burning, but is not absolutely necessary.

A variety of fuel from small sticks to large logs, is fed into the hole, where it burns down to form a layer of glowing coals. Additional wood should be kept burning outside the hole and the coals it produces shoveled in as needed.

In Mexico the meat to be barbecued was often wrapped in maguey (century plant) leaves, beaten to make them flexible. There is little maguey in Texas so they improvise with wet gunny sacks. The meat, rubbed with salt and wrapped in a clean cloth and the wet sacks, is placed on top, and the hole is covered with earth and left to cook for at least eight hours, sometimes overnight.

Even the toughest meat comes out deliciously tender, with a unique, delightful flavor. Sometimes an earthen pot of beans or garbanzos (chick-peas) and water is put in the hole along with the meat to bake slowly.

Any kind of meat can be cooked in this traditional way, but the ancient offering is the head of a steer or calf. Sometimes the Indians and the early Texas settlers used a buffalo head instead.

The horns were cut off and the head was skinned and washed. Sometimes hot chilies were put in the mouth. Setting the entire head on the table was usually not recommended. The cooked meat, including the tongue and brains, was separated from the skull and arranged on a serving platter. The skull was quietly slipped from view.

A FEW WORDS ABOUT BARBEQUING

Both regular charcoal briquets and mesquite charcoal are good fuels for grilling. Mesquite charcoal burns hotter than regular charcoal and gives foods like grilled fish and poultry a smokier flavor.

Mesquite coals aren't uniformly shaped; they range in size from tiny shards to 4-inch chunks. The fire will be hotter where large lumps poke upward, so break up big pieces for more even heat.

Another outdoor cooking method gaining popularity is the gas grill. For most cooking jobs the gas grill is best, because it offers excellent heat control. Mesquite chips can be moistened and sprinkled onto the lava rocks to add the distinctive mesquite flavor. For some recipes, especially those requiring extra-long cooking times, a large outdoor pit is the only way to BBQ and properly smoke the meat.

Three different terms are commonly used to indicate desired cooking temperature.

• Hot describes coals that are barely covered with gray ash. You can hold your hand near the grill for only 2 to 3 seconds. Hot also describes the upper third of the gas BBQ's thermometer range. The thermometer is usually in the lid or cover. It takes 10 to 15 minutes for a gas BBQ to get this hot.

• Medium describes coals that glow through a layer of gray ash. You can hold your hand near the grill for only 4 to 5 seconds. When your gas BBQ's thermometer is in the middle of its range, it has reached medium heat.

• Low describes coals covered with a thick layer of gray ash. You should be able to hold your hand near the grill for 6 to 7 seconds. A gas BBQ is at low heat when its thermometer is in the lower third of its range.

~~~~~~

SETTING UP YOUR GRILL

Grease grill lightly, a non-stick spray works best, and set in place at the recommended height (3 to 5 inches) above the coals. Allow the BBQ to reach the proper temperature. Arrange food on the grill. If you are using an uncovered grill, you can get better results by covering as much of the grill area as possible. A covered BBQ produces the best results because it holds the heat and flavorful smoke in. Watch carefully and turn as needed to ensure even cooking. It's best to avoid sauce that's high in sugar or fat, but if you do, apply it during the last part of cooking and turn food often to prevent scorching. A water-filled spray bottle works well to extinguish flare-ups.

DIRECT HEAT

Direct heat is good for burgers, chops, steaks, poultry pieces, or any small pieces of meat. Open the bottom dampers if your barbecue has them. Arrange the briquettes on the fire grate in a solid layer that's 1 to 2 inches bigger all around than the grill area needed for the food. Then build a pyramid shaped pile of briquets and ignite it. When the coals have reached the heat condition specified in the recipe, spread them out into a single layer again. For gas BBQ's, set the flame on high and preheat to hot.

INDIRECT HEAT

Indirect heat is suitable for whole fish as well as roasts, whole poultry, and other food that requires long cooking times.

Open or remove lid from a covered barbecue, and open the bottom dampers. Place 50 long-burning briquets on the fire grate and ignite. Let them burn for about 30 minutes or until hot.

With long-handled tongs, bank half the briquets on each side of grate and place a metal drip pan in the center. Grease grill lightly and place the grill 4 to 6 inches above pan. In a gas BBQ, indirect heat can be achieved by pre-heating the grill to hot, and then turning the gas down very low for cooking.

Arrange the food directly above drip pan. If you're grilling meat, place it fat side up. Marinated meat should be drained before grilling. Cover barbecue and adjust dampers as necessary to maintain an even heat. Add 5 or 6 briquets to each side of grate at 30 to 40 minute intervals as needed to keep fire temperature constant.

SMOKE/INDIRECT

Some BBQ recipes call for very slow cooking and/or smoking. This process can take up to ten hours or more. The secret to this method is two-fold: one is the tenderness achieved by very slow cooking, the other is the flavor added by the smoke. The smoke flavor comes from two sources, the wood smoke, and the vaporized drippings and fat.

Slow cooking and smoking requires control of the dampers and vent locations to cause the smoke and heat from the coals to flow across the meat. This means that you must arrange your BBQ so that air comes in under the coals, travels across the meat, and exits on the opposite side of the grill. In this method, the coals or hardwood are never directly under the food, but rather to one side, that opposite the flue. A drip pan with a little water is placed under the meat, next to the coals, to catch the drippings. Let the drippings simmer to help produce that unique barbeque flavor.

You can also achieve this in a gas grill that has two burners. After pre-heating the grill to hot, turn the flame down very low and place the meat above the second burner, with only the primary burner lit. Then cook slowly with the lid down. Mesquite or hardwood chips (slightly dampened) can be sprinkled on the lava rock over the burning side, to add that wood smoke flavor.

Although slow-cooking and smoking are more difficult and time-consuming, old time chefs swear by these methods and claim that they produce the best results.

STEAK SECRETS

Here are a few suggestions for barbequing great steaks!

A clean grill will stick to food less.

Trim fat from meat so the drippings won't flare-up as much. If the drippings flare up during cooking, use a spray bottle with water to cool the flare-up. Slice 1/8-inch or so into edges of the meat to prevent cupping.

Pre-heat your grill to hot, with the lid or cover on. The high heat will seal-in the juices at the very beginning before any are lost. Turn onto an unused area of grill after about a minute to seal the other side. At this point you can season, salt and pepper. If you salt uncooked meat, you can dry it out.

When little pools of juice form on the top, the meat is ready to turn again. Splash that juice onto other just-turned pieces to add flavor.

Always turn your meat with tongs. Piercing with a fork leaks precious juices.

Broil the second side a few minutes less than the first.

Carve a big steak, like a porterhouse or a sirloin, so that everyone can share the choice portions. Remove the bone, cutting very close to it. Then cut across the full width of the steak, making 1-inch slices and narrowing them toward the tenderloin.

BUCKAROO FILETS

Flatten minute steaks and spread one side lightly with prepared mustard. At narrow end of each, place a strip of dill pickle or candied dill pickle, or 1 or 2 green onions. Roll up, starting at end with pickle. Fasten with small metal skewers or toothpicks; brush outside with melted butter or margarine. Broil on grill over hot coals 10 to 15 minutes, turning once. When done to your liking, sprinkle with salt and pepper.

The mustard adds a great flavor. And rolling up the slim minute steaks keeps them juicy.

SPIT ROASTED
STUFFED FLANK STEAK

1 to 1-1/4-pound flank steak
1/2 teaspoon non-seasoned meat tenderizer
2 tablespoons prepared mustard
1-1/2 cups dry bread cubes
1/2 cup chopped onion
1/2 cup chopped celery
3 tablespoons melted butter
1/2 teaspoon poultry seasoning
1/4 teaspoon salt
Garlic or clear French dressing

Score steak on both sides with a meat tenderizer. Spread one side of steak with mustard. Combine bread, onion, celery, butter and seasonings for stuffing and spread over steak.

Roll like a jellyroll and fasten meat with skewers or toothpicks. Lace with string. Balance meat on spit, insert holding forks. Attach spit and turn on motor. Baste with garlic dressing. Roast over medium coals about 35 minutes or till done, basting frequently with garlic dressing. Serves 4 or 5.

SHOESTRING STEAK BARBECUE

4 pounds round steak
1 tablespoon Worcestershire sauce
1/2 cup olive oil
1/2 cup flour
pepper and salt

Slice round steak very thin, then cut into shoestrings. With a very sharp knife and a good cutting board you will be able to slice strips 1/8 inch in cross section. Form into patties. Dip in olive oil and then in flour. Sprinkle with Worcestershire sauce and pepper. Broil over hardwood coals. The lean meat will drip far less than hamburger, while the olive oil will impart a subtly delicious flavor. Salt when finished. Shoestring Steaks are best served a little rare.

SPIT ROASTED BARBECUED SPARERIBS WITH RED SAUCE

4 pounds spareribs, in 4 pieces, trimmed of excess fat
1/2 cup vegetable oil
3 cups coarsely chopped onions
1 tablespoon finely chopped garlic
1 pound can tomatoes, drained
and coarsely chopped with the liquid reserved
1 cup canned tomato puree
1/4 cup fresh hot red chilies including the seeds
2 tablespoons dry mustard
2 tablespoons sugar
1 tablespoon distilled white vinegar
1-1/2 teaspoons salt

Prepare the red sauce as follows: In a heavy 10 to 12 inch skillet, heat the vegetable oil over moderate heat. Add the onions and garlic while stirring frequently and cook for about 5 minutes, or until they are soft and translucent but not brown. Coarsely chop the chilies. Stir in the tomatoes and their liquid, the tomato puree, chilies, mustard, sugar, vinegar and salt, and bring to a boil over high heat. Cook briskly, uncovered, until the sauce is thick enough to hold its shape almost solidly in the spoon. Remove the pan from the heat and taste the red sauce for seasoning. Set it aside.

For barbecuing the ribs, light a 2-inch-thick layer of charcoal briquettes in a charcoal grill equipped with a rotating spit. Let the coals burn until you have a low temperature, direct heat fire as described at the beginning of this chapter.

Thread the spareribs on the spit, running the spit through the meat over and under alternate pairs of ribs. Then secure them at both ends with the sliding prongs. Fit the spit into place about 6 inches above the surface of the coals and barbecue the ribs for 45 minutes, or until they are lightly and evenly browned. Watch carefully for any sign of burning and regulate the height of the spit accordingly.

With a pastry brush, spread the red sauce evenly on both sides of the spareribs. Basting the ribs every 5 minutes or so, continue to barbecue them for about 30 minutes longer, or until they are richly colored and glazed with sauce.

To serve, remove the spit from the grill, unscrew the prongs and slide the spareribs off the spit onto a heated platter. Before serving, insert skewers into each section of ribs if you like.

Santa Fe Bob Sez:

Some towns in the Old West owned barbecue spits made to specifications by blacksmiths. These had cranks to be turned by one or two men, and were mounted on bearings, generally from discarded wagon wheels. Often they were constructed of items on hand such as log chains and pulleys. In order to shorten the cooking process, a sheet metal hood was set over the beef to keep the heat in. A barbeque was often a big community event with many townspeople involved. The pit tenders had to keep constant vigil throughout the night to insure the success of the main course.

Steaks, a cowboy favorite, were usually fried using a heavy griddle over a campfire. But, broiling meat over hardwood coals was a tasty, though more involved, method closer to our modern conception of barbeque. Roasting sticks were wrapped with strips of salt pork then steaks were secured around the pork with wire or wet twine. The sticks were then propped over the flames. The flames enhanced the flavor and if the meat caught on fire it was removed and laid briefly in the grass.

~~~~~~

WHOLE STEER BARBEQUE

whole steer
1/2 pound pepper
2 pounds. of salt
2 pounds of lard

The steer must be specially handled when butchered and hung in one piece. Save the hide but have the hair removed. After the steer has been properly aged, mount it whole on a steel bar or pipe which will be the spit. The spit should be twice as long as the animal. Lay the steer on its back and place the spit down the abdominal cavity making sure to find the center of balance so that turning during roasting will not be difficult. Using wet rope or flexible wire fasten the beef tight, close the abdomen and rub a mixture of salt, lard, and pepper all over. Once you have done that, sew the hide back around it.

The cookfire can be built on the ground, but long pans for coals or grates for the wood are much better. Build the fire with two long fire-pans on either side of a third pan to catch the drippings. A bucket of water should be kept nearby to fill the drip pan and extinguish flames. Some of the drippings and fat will fall into the fire, but you want to avoid that because the smoke is unpleasant and it will affect the quality of the meat. Go a dozen steps away from your pit and put down a metal plate or some sort of fireproof slab you can shovel from. Build your fire. Be sure to have plenty of hardwood (as much as a cord for a whole steer) or anthracite coal. Mount the beef in your pit. When coals are formed, move them a shovelful at a time to the fire-pans. Keep the heat going without interruption. Barbequing a steer takes all night and into the next day with constant attention. When the drippings collect they should be used to baste the meat along with the special barbeque sauce (recipe below). Be sure to give it one complete revolution per hour. When meat starts to pull back from the bones it's approaching the eating stage. The hide will shrivel, curl back and become very hard. To test make a deep cut in the sirloin. The middle should be rare. Remove from fire and cut away the hide. Place beef back down, remove from spit, and cut in half down the spine with a meat clever. Cut into the hindquarters and remove the shanks. To carve, start with the lower round and prime rib. Progress to the front quarter from the prime rib to the shoulder and neck, while carving on the hindquarter moves from the shank round to the T-bone, making sure that the last person in line is equal to the first.

BARBEQUE SAUCE

1 cup blackstrap molasses
1/2 cup black pepper
1 cup vinegar
1 pound salt
stale beer as needed
1 quart olive oil

Mix all the ingredients except the stale beer, then add the beer until a mixture is obtained which is thin enough to drip from a brush, but not so thin as to repel the olive oil when it is stirred. Apply this sauce alternately with the meat drippings as described in the whole steer barbeque recipe above.

QUICK SMOKED BEANS

4 ounces salt pork, cut in l-inch cubes
2 1-pound cans (4 cups) pork and beans
1/2 cup catsup
1/4 cup brown sugar
1 teaspoon dry mustard

Brown salt pork in skillet and drain. In 2-quart bean pot, combine remaining ingredients. Top with salt pork. Bake uncovered on grill of hickory-smoker with hood down, 1 hour or longer. You can also cook in a barbeque grill with moistened mesquite chips. Serves 8.

RANCHER'S GRILLED CHUCK STEAK

1/2 cup chopped onion
1/2 cup lemon juice
1/4 cup salad oil
1/2 teaspoon salt
1/2 teaspoon celery salt
1/2 teaspoon pepper
1/2 teaspoon thyme
1/2 teaspoon oregano
1/2 teaspoon rosemary
1 clove garlic, minced
2-1/2 pounds chuck steak, 2-1/2-inches thick

Combine all ingredients except steak in a shallow ceramic dish to make marinade. Add meat to mixture and marinate for 3 hours in refrigerator, turning several times. Drain. Broil steak on grill over hot coals. Cook steak to doneness you like (about 30 minutes total time), turning once. Baste with marinade during broiling. Makes about 4 servings.

CHUCK WAGON BEANS

2 cups dry navy beans
1-1/2 quarts cold water
1 teaspoon salt
1/4 pound salt pork, diced
1-1/2 teaspoons salt
1/2 teaspoon dry mustard
1/4 cup granulated or brown sugar
2 tablespoons molasses
1 small onion, quartered

Rinse beans; cover with the cold water. Bring to boiling and simmer 2 minutes. Remove from heat. Cover; let stand 1 hour or overnight. Add 1 teaspoon salt to beans and soaking water, cover and simmer until just tender, about 45 minutes to 1 hour. Drain, reserving liquid.

Place half the beans in Dutch oven. Bury part of pork in beans. Combine the remaining ingredients and add half. Add remaining beans and seasonings Place remaining salt pork over top. Cover with bean liquid. Cover Dutch oven and bury in coals of campfire or bake in oven at low heat for 6 to 8 hours. If necessary, add more liquid as beans bake.

For smoky flavor: If you have a covered grill, you can cook the last 2 or 3 hours on grill. Just uncover beans and toss hickory or mesquite chips on coals. Or add liquid smoke in the last hour of cooking.

CHINESE SMOKED RIBS

6 pounds loin back ribs or spareribs

Ginger Sauce:
1/2 cup soy sauce
1/2 cup catsup
1/4 cup water
3 tablespoons brown sugar
2 tablespoons grated fresh ginger root
or 2 teaspoons ground ginger
Barbecue Rub:
2 tablespoons sugar
1/2 teaspoon salt
1/4 teaspoon each paprika,
turmeric, and celery seed
dash dry mustard

For Ginger Sauce, mix first 6 ingredients and let stand overnight to mellow the flavor. For Barbecue Rub, combine sugar and seasonings. Rub the ribs with this mixture; let stand 2 hours. Brush with Ginger Sauce and let stand about 30 minutes to 1 hour.

Hang the ribs in a smoker oven which uses wood as fuel (oak, hickory, or fruitwood). Smoke spareribs about 1-1/2 hours or loin back ribs about 2 hours, or till done, brushing occasionally with the sauce. Keep fire at about 325°F. Snip ribs into serving pieces.

CHICKEN ESCABECHE

2-1/2 tablespoons Escabeche Paste (recipe follows)
3-1/2 to 4 pound frying chickens, cut up
1 -1/2 cups regular-strength chicken broth
1 tablespoon vegetable oil
2 large onions, thinly sliced
1 can (7 oz.) diced green chilies
1-1/2 tablespoons cornstarch
mixed with 1-1/2 tablespoons water
3 tablespoons chopped fresh cilantro

Prepare Escabeche Paste. Rinse chicken, pat dry and cut into pieces. Pierce chicken all over then rub on paste, pushing some under skin. Place chicken in a 9 x 13 inch baking pan. Pour in broth, cover and bake in a 400°F. oven until chicken is tender when pierced (about 40 minutes).

Lift chicken from broth and drain. Skim and discard fat from broth and reserve. Place chicken on a lightly greased grill 4 to 6 inches above a solid bed of medium coals. Cook, turning as needed, until well browned. In a large frying pan over medium heat, add onions to oil and cook until soft. Stir in chilies, reserved broth, and cornstarch mixture. Cook, stirring, until sauce boils and thickens. Stir in cilantro. Spoon sauce onto individual portions of chicken. Makes 4 or 5 servings.

ESCABECHE PASTE

8 cloves garlic, minced or pressed
1 teaspoon each allspice, cloves, cumin, and coriander.
1-1/2 teaspoons ground cinnamon
3/4 teaspoon coarsely ground pepper
2 teaspoons dry oregano leaves
1/4 teaspoon cayenne pepper
2 tablespoons each orange juice and white wine vinegar.

Thoroughly mix together all dry ingredients then add juice and vinegar Use, or cover and refrigerate for up to 2 weeks. Makes 1/4 cup.

ROASTED SALSA SPARERIBS

The barbecue does double duty when you prepare these tasty pork ribs. Start by charring tomatoes and green chilies to make a tart salsa. Then grill the ribs using the salsa as a basting sauce.

6 large, firm-ripe tomatoes
8 large fresh mild green chilies (such as Anaheim)
1/4 cup each red wine vinegar and chopped cilantro
3 cloves garlic, minced or pressed
salt
6 to 8 pounds pork spareribs
1 cup sour cream
4 limes

Prepare a low heat fire according to directions at the beginning of this chapter. Mound and ignite 50 charcoal briquets. When coals are heavily spotted with gray ash spread to make an even layer

Set tomatoes and chilies on a lightly greased grill to 6 inches above prepared coals. Cook, turning as needed, until chilies are charred on all sides (7 to 10 minutes) and tomatoes are hot and streaked with brown (about 15 minutes).

Using long tongs, mound hot charcoal for barbecuing by indirect cooking method. Place a shallow metal drip pan in center then add 5 fresh briquets to each side.

To make the salsa, chop grilled tomatoes and chilies discarding stems and seeds. Place tomatoes and chilies and their juices in a bowl. Stir in vinegar, cilantro, garlic; season to taste with salt. Spread some of the salsa evenly over both sides of ribs.

Place ribs, meat side up, on grill directly above drip pan (overlap ribs to fit on grill if necessary). Cover barbecue and adjust dampers as necessary to maintain an even heat. Cook, basting occasionally with some of the remaining salsa, until meat near bone is no longer pink; cut to test (1 to 1-1/4 hours). To serve, cut ribs into 2- to 3-rib portions; garnish with lime slices, if desired. Serve with remaining salsa, cream, and lime wedges.

TAOS GRILLED TURKEY

10 to 12 pound turkey
4 to 6 limes, cut in half
4 teaspoons dry oregano leaves
salt and pepper

Remove turkey neck, giblets, and any large lumps of fat. Rinse and pat dry.

Before cooking, squeeze 1 or 2 lime halves and rub over turkey and inside cavities; sprinkle with oregano, then lightly sprinkle with salt and pepper inside and out. Insert a meat thermometer into the thickest part of the thigh making sure it does not touch the bone.

Barbecue turkey by indirect heat (see Salsa Sparerib recipe, previous page), placing turkey, breast up, on grill directly above drip pan. Cover barbecue and adjust dampers as necessary to maintain an even heat. Cook turkey until meat thermometer registers 185°F or until meat near thighbone is no longer pink (cut to test)—about 3 hours. Every 30 minutes, squeeze 1 or 2 lime halves and rub over turkey.

Transfer turkey to a platter and carve in the usual manner. Makes about 12 servings.

PEPPER CHICKEN WITH LIME

3 frying chickens, 2 to 2-1/2 pounds each
juice of 3 limes
1 cup virgin olive oil
1 large onion, finely chopped
3 large garlic cloves, minced
1/4 cup crushed dried red chile
1-1/2 teaspoons salt
1 teaspoon oregano

Rinse the chickens and remove any pinfeathers and excess skin and fat. Cut into quarters. You can remove the skin at this time if desired. Place chicken in a large glass baking dish.

Mix the remaining ingredients together and generously baste both sides of each chicken quarter. Cover and set aside for 1 hour.

Build a low heat fire in the grill soon after you've finished preparing chicken. If using mesquite wood chips or any other type of aromatic enhancer, soak them at this time for applying when you distribute the coals. When the coals are whitish gray, scatter them evenly in a circle large enough to cook all the chicken. First, lightly coat grill with Pam or other spray-on oil so chicken doesn't stick to grill. Place the grill about 5 inches above the bed of coals and allow to heat thoroughly.

Place the chicken pieces on the grill, skin side down. Watch the grilling carefully; if there are any flareups, extinguish them with a water sprayer. Chicken with skin removed will not flareup as much, but you must remember to watch it carefully as it will cook faster. Turn the chicken pieces frequently for the most flavorful and juicy result.

The chicken is done when the leg and thigh pieces can easily be bent at the joint. This should take about 45 minutes (less for skinless). Remove and keep warm. Serves 12.

~~~~~~

BARBECUED BEEF BRISKET for 50
OVEN METHOD

Assuming you probably don't take your barbecuing quite as seriously as those Old West cooks who used to tend their pits night and day before a big barbeque, here's a fabulous-tasting barbecued brisket for a large party that can be done in your oven. It's easy to scale the proportions to prepare for a smaller number.

25 pounds beef brisket
1-1/2 cups liquid hickory smoke
12 onions, chopped medium fine
1-1/2 cups cider vinegar
1-1/2 cups dark brown sugar, firmly packed
3/4 cup strong, spicy dark mustard
3/4 cup dark molasses
1-1/2 teaspoons cayenne pepper
Several drops of liquid hot pepper sauce, to taste
1-1/4 cups Worcestershire sauce
1-1/2 quarts ketchup
3 cups commercial chili sauce (tomato based)
3 lemons
1/4 cup salt, or to taste
1 tablespoon freshly ground black pepper

Place the meat, fat side up, on a trivet or baking rack in a large roaster. Place the liquid smoke in the bottom of the pan, rubbing the outside of the meat with a little of the smoke. Cover and roast at 325°F for 6 hours, or until very tender. Turn after 3 hours. For the last hour, remove the lid to allow the roast to brown. Test for tenderness—it should almost fall apart.

Remove from the oven and allow to cool. Seal in a plastic, stainless steel, or glass container and refrigerate overnight. Place the pan juices and fat in a separate container.

The next day, trim away any excess fat. Then shred the beef by pulling it with two meat forks and your hands. Separate it into short shreds making sure that none are over 3 inches.

Lift off the hardened fat from the pan juices and place it back in the roasting pan. (Use only a generous cupful, discarding the rest of the fat, but reserving the juices.) Melt the fat, placing the roaster on a burner. Add the chopped onion and cook and stir until the onion becomes limp. Thinly slice lemons into complete rounds, skin and all, removing ends and seeds. Then add lemons and all the remaining ingredients. Simmer 30 minutes.

Add the beef to the sauce, stirring as you add it. Simmer uncovered very slowly, either on the stovetop or place it back in a 325°F. oven. Stir frequently. Add the reserved pan juices as it cooks down, being careful not to get it too soupy. Once all the pan juices have been added, add water to keep the meat moist. Simmer at least 1 hour before serving. The meat actually improves while setting at low heat, so it makes a great buffet dish.

Serve as is, or with soft buns or cornbread for making sandwiches.

BASIC DRY RUB FOR BARBECUE

3 tablespoons salt
3 tablespoons black pepper
3 tablespoons paprika

For ribs you may add:
1 tablespoon lemon powder
6 tablespoons sugar
(Remember to watch for flame-ups if you choose to add sugar—it burns)

For chicken you may add to the basic rub:
2 tablespoons garlic powder
2 tablespoons dry mustard
1 teaspoon crumbled bay leaf

REAL TEXAS BARBECUE

*Texans would like to be known as the barbeque experts. However, there is much disagreement about the proper way to barbeque even among the Texans. There is one school of thought that says **wet sauces are bad for barbecue**. This theory is based on the fact that any sauce with tomato or sugar will burn. Barbecue cooked dry— over a very low heat and in a covered barbecue pit—will produce a marvelous "real" Texas barbecue.*

This is what the experts say about cooking a brisket: Choose about a 9-pound beef brisket. Be sure to choose one with a little fat on it. The flavor won't be as good if it is too lean.

Make the basic dry rub (see recipe previous page)—and rub thoroughly all over the meat. Don't ever pierce the meat with a fork. Turn with a tongs.

Prepare a fire for smoke/indirect cooking as described at the beginning of this chapter, using mesquite, hickory, or oak. If you have to you can use wood chips soaked in water with charcoal. Now let your fire burn down real low.

Your fire shouldn't be too hot. But you can't let it go out either. You may have to nurse it along, adding small logs or charcoal from time to time. Remember to keep the fire off the meat. Keep water nearby to quench any flame-ups.

When your fire is burning just right, put the brisket on and cover it up. A 9-pound brisket should cook about 18 hours for that real Texas barbeque flavor. Be sure to keep a close watch. Turn the meat once in awhile with the tongs and add wood to the fire or water to the pan.

VARIATIONS: You can do the same thing with pork ribs, chicken, or steak. Use the dry rub seasonings (see recipes previous page). Cook ribs about 3 hours, chicken about 2, steak just 20 minutes.

RIBS AND BARBEQUE MOP

For this technique it is important to remember that if the fire is too hot you will burn the ribs to a crisp. Be stingy with the fire. Just a little heat, a lot of smoke, mop and turn the ribs regularly, and by dinnertime you'll have the best barbecued ribs you ever ate. This method works for beef and chicken, too.

After building a low fire according to the smoke/indirect cooking method described at the beginning of this chapter, put on a side of pork ribs to cook and begin mopping each side with the mop sauce (see recipe below). This method requires constant attention. About every 20 minutes, mop the ribs, and turn them. After 4 hours, the ribs should be done. To test, take a pair of kitchen tongs and lift up one end of the ribs. The meat should be very flexible and bend almost double without threatening to break.

Some people say cooking ribs by this method is crazy. It couldn't possibly take 4 hours to cook little skinny ribs. You'll just have to give this method a try and taste the ribs for yourself.

BARBEQUE MOP

1-1/2 teaspoon salt
1-1/2 teaspoon dry mustard
1 teaspoon garlic powder
1/2 teaspoon ground bay leaf
1 teaspoon chile powder
1-1/2 teaspoon paprika
1 teaspoon Louisiana Hot Sauce
2/3 cup Worcestershire sauce
1/3 cup apple cider vinegar
2-2/3 cup beef stock
1/3 cup vegetable oil

Combine all ingredients and use to mop meats that are barbecuing. To make a mop, you can use a dime-store dish mop or you can make one at home by using a long-handled wooden spoon and some clean rags which you tie to the end of the spoon with string. Some people prefer the rag version because they can just throw the rags away when the barbeque is finished. Leftover sauce will keep well in the refrigerator.

During the barbeque, you will notice that as you stick the mop in the sauce the color darkens and becomes more chocolate brown because meat juices are blending with the sauce. This enhances the flavor of the sauce and will make it better the second time you use it. You can use this mop for beef, pork, or chicken with equally good results.

As you can see, this sauce has no tomato and no sugar. Any so-called barbecue sauce with tomato or sugar should be served on the side and not rubbed on cooking meat because sugar or tomato will burn and char the meat surface. Always read labels on commercial products and apply the same rule. Makes 1 quart.

TEXAS TABLE SAUCE
FOR BARBECUE

No matter how you are barbequing, with a dry seasoning and/or with the mop sauce, you may still wish to serve a sauce at the table. To get good smokey flavor in a table sauce, cook it on the edge of the grill for an hour or so while the barbecue is going. Cooking the sauce outside will produce the desired effect. You may notice a few ashes floating up into the sauce. No, problem! Just stir them in. If you want to make this sauce on the stovetop, add a little artificial smoke if you like, but don't compare it to sauce cooked outside.

3/4 cup cider vinegar
3/4 cup warm water
1 tablespoon salt
1 teaspoon coarsely ground pepper
1 teaspoon Hungarian paprika

2 tablespoons dark brown sugar
1 tablespoon dark molasses
3 tablespoons dry mustard
1/2 cup catsup
1/4 cup chile sauce
3 tablespoons Worcestershire sauce
1 clove garlic, pressed
2 tablespoons onion, finely minced
1 cup butter or margarine

In a bowl, combine vinegar and water. Stir in salt, pepper, paprika, brown sugar, molasses, and dry mustard. Set aside to steep. Combine catsup, chili sauce, Worcestershire sauce, garlic, onion, and butter in medium saucepan. Raise to a boil over medium-low heat. Stir in vinegar/water mixture.

Transfer to your outdoor cooker and simmer uncovered for 1 hour or so, stirring from time to time. If cooked indoors, simmer about 30 minutes. Serve hot with your favorite barbequed dishes.

This sauce will keep well in the refrigerator. You can use it for oven barbecuing if you keep the temperature low (about 275°F.), and cover the meat, but never use this sauce for outside barbecuing. It will char meat because it contains both sugar and tomatoes. Makes enough for 6 pounds of meat.

GRILLED HERBED TROUT

Before grilling, these trout soak up flavor in an herbed marinade and when grilled are very tender. Serve with Citrus Salsa or Jalapeño Mayonnaise (see recipes in Fruits and Meats and Main Courses chapters).

> *4 whole trout (about 1/2 pound each)*
> *2/3 cup vegetable oil*
> *1/4 cup white wine vinegar*
> *1/2 teaspoon each dry basil and dry oregano leaves*
> *1 clove garlic, minced or pressed*
> *1/4 teaspoon each salt and pepper*
> *green onions and oranges for garnish*

Clean fish, rinse and pat dry. Leave whole or bone and butterfly. To bone cleaned trout and keep head and tail in place, open body cavity; insert a sharp knife at head end under backbone and cut between ribs and flesh. Repeat process to free other side. Cut underneath backbone to free. Using kitchen scissors, snip backbone at head and tail; lift out and discard. Cut off and discard fins. Spread fish out flat.

In a shallow ceramic dish, stir together oil, vinegar, basil, oregano, garlic, salt, and pepper. Add fish to oil mixture; turn to coat. Cover and refrigerate for 1 to 2 hours, turning once. Meanwhile, prepare Citrus Salsa and Jalapeño Mayonnaise; cover and refrigerate.

Lift fish from marinade and drain briefly (discard marinade). Barbecue whole fish by the indirect cooking method as described at the beginning of this chapter by placing fish on grill directly above drip pan. Place boned fish on a well-greased grill 4 to 6 inches above a solid bed of hot coals.

Cook whole or boned fish, turning once, just until fish flakes when prodded with a fork in thickest part (10 to 12 minutes for whole fish, 6 to 8 minutes for boned fish). With two metal spatulas, carefully transfer cooked trout to a warm rimmed platter. Garnish with whole grilled green onions and orange slices. Serve with Citrus Salsa and Jalapeño Mayonnaise.

Santa Fe Bob sez:

From their humble beginnings fajitas have caught on like fire fanning out from South Texas. Farm laborers along the border prepared fajitas for themselves from the trimmings their bosses gave them. Fajitas are made from relatively inexpensive skirt steak (the belly trimmings) or bottom round, which must be cut very thin. The authentic smoky flavor comes from marinating the beef in lime juice and garlic and grilling it over mesquite. Fajitas are traditionally served on sizzling steak platters on top of warm flour tortillas, sauced with peppery hot Pico de Gallo and sour cream.

Pico de Gallo or "Cock's comb" is a southeastern Texas border sauce borrowed from northern Mexico. The traditional accompaniment to Fajitas, it is also an excellent spicy red table sauce. Although chipotle (smoked jalapenos) are the traditional ingredient you can substitute jalapeño and some pequin or caribe. If you have access to chipotles be sure to use them.

MESQUITE-GRILLED FAJITAS

3 pounds skirt steak or very lean round steak
2 limes
6 garlic cloves, minced
1 teaspoon salt
freshly ground black pepper to taste
6 to 8 large 12-inch flour tortillas
12 to 16 leaves of rinsed, whole romaine lettuce
Pico de Gallo Sauce (recipe follows)
8 ounces sour cream
2 ripe avocados

Trim the steaks, removing any fat and sinew. Pound as thin as possible. Cut into strips 4 to 6 inches long by 2 inches wide.

Squeeze the limes and combine the juice with the garlic, salt, and a generous amount of pepper. Place steak in a shallow bowl, then thoroughly cover steak pieces with the lime mixture. Let set at room temperature for at least 30 minutes, preferably for 2 hours.

About 45 minutes before serving, prepare a hot fire for direct cooking method as described at the beginning of this chapter, using mesquite to flavor the charcoal briquets.

Grill should be about 3 to 4 inches from the coals. Grill strips until charred on each side, but still rare in the center. Heat foil wrapped flour tortillas for 15 minutes in a 350°F. oven, or heat tortillas on the grill.

To serve, place a piece of steak in the center of each tortilla, with a piece of romaine on either side.

For those who like it hot, spoon a little Pico de Gallo on the inside. Wrap and serve with sour cream and sliced avocados on the side. You should also drizzle a little Pico de Gallo over the top.

PICO DE GALLO SAUCE

3 fresh jalapenos, finely chopped (about 1/2 cup)
1 large red, ripe unpeeled tomato, coarsely chopped

1 medium white onion, coarsely chopped (about 1/2 cup)
2 garlic cloves, minced
1/2 teaspoon salt
1/2 teaspoon pequin or caribe (or to taste)
3 tablespoons coarsely chopped fresh cilantro

Combine all the ingredients and allow to marinate and develop natural juices for at least 1 hour before serving.

BARBEQUED MARINATED RABBIT

Rinse rabbit pieces and pat dry. Arrange in a single layer in a shallow dish. Prepare Paprika Marinade; pour over rabbit. Cover and refrigerate for at least 1 hour or until next day, turning occasionally.

Lift rabbit from marinade and drain briefly (reserve marinade). Barbecue rabbit by indirect heat, placing rabbit on grill directly above drip pan. Cover barbecue and adjust dampers as necessary to maintain an even heat. Cook, basting often with marinade, until meat is white at bone. Cut to test after about 35 minutes. Makes 4 or 5 servings.

PAPRIKA MARINADE

1/2 cup vegetable oil
1/4 cup red wine vinegar
2 tablespoons paprika
1 tablespoon Worcestershire
1 clove garlic, minced or pressed.

Combine all the ingredients and allow to marinate and develop natural juices for at least 1 hour before serving.

Chili, Soups,
and Stews

Because of the limited and unsophisticated kitchen utensils available in the Old West, many foods were cooked in large pots or Dutch ovens. These big cast-iron covered pots were used for everything from a batch of chili or stew to baking bread. But there is no question that the favorite "mess" was something with a little meat, some beans or some vegetables. Because dried beans could be kept in just a burlap sack for months or even years, they were used extensively to supply chuckwagons and the larders of many pioneers and ranchers. It was this universality of beans, along with the influence of Mexican cooking, that gave birth to modern chili. In Texas, chili is somewhat of an art form, but these concoctions are still basically a little meat, some beans and some chilies.

Here's an old chili blessing from a cowpuncher:

"Lord, God, You know us old cowhands is forgetful.
Sometimes I can't even recollect what happened yestiddy.
We is forgetful. We just know daylight and dark,
summer, fall, winter and spring. But I sure hope we don't
never forget to thank You before we is about to eat a
mess of good chili. We don't know why, in Your wisdom,
You been so doggone good to us. The Chinee don't have
no chili, ever. The Frenchmens is left out. The Rooshians
don't know no more about chili than a hog does about a
sidesaddle. Even the Meskins don't get a good whiff of it
unless they stay around here. Chili eaters is
some of Your chosen people .... Amen."

That old cowpuncher didn't know that sections of China are similar to areas of Southwest Texas, and "The Chinee" were cooking with hot peppers long before he was born.

The most famous of all chili dishes is chili con carne, which is something of an obsession in Texas. Nowadays, chili-cooking contests all over the Southwest attract thousands of fans. One thing that Texas chili lovers want to make clear is that the celebrated chili con carne is not a Mexican invention. There is little hard evidence to prove this, but it is equally hard to disprove.

It is true, however, that the Indians of the American Southwest were making concoctions of chilies and meat long before Columbus and Cortez. Shortly after the first Spaniards entered Mexico City, they described the thousands of dishes that consisted of chilies cooked with what must have been every kind of meat, fish or fowl available to the Aztecs. And in modern Mexico, women stand in the great markets beside simmering pots of chili peppers cooked with all sorts of ingredients. When these stews contain a substantial amount of meat, they are essentially chili con came.

In spite of this, it's likely that Texas-style chili con carne, was invented somewhere in Texas, possibly in San Antonio. It is not very liquid, as the Mexican market stews generally are, and its main ingredient is beef, which is too expensive in Mexico to be eaten in quantity by many of the people who frequent the markets. A fair compromise might be to say that chili con carne is a Texas dish inspired by Mexico. It is, in other words, an ideal example of "Tex-Mex," or Texas-Mexican cooking.

HOW TO HANDLE CHILIES

Hot peppers, or chilies, vary in hotness—sometimes even on a single plant. Fresh green chilies are under ripe red chilies, and taste almost the same. Canned green chilies are mild; canned jalapeno chilies are very hot. Though most dried chilies are hot, the Ancho variety is almost sweet and is used primarily to give sauces a maroon color.

The volatile oils in all chilies may burn your skin and eyes. Wearing rubber gloves is an excellent precaution, and you should be careful not to touch your face while working with chilies. After handling chilies, wash your hands (and the gloves) thoroughly with soap and water.

Before cutting chilies, rinse them clean and pull out the stems under cold running water. Cut the pods in half and remove the seeds. They may be used at once or soaked in cold salted water for an hour or so to make them milder.

Small dried chilies should be stemmed, broken open and seeded before they are used. Dried ancho chilies should be plumped as well. Place the seeded ancho chilies in a bowl, pour in enough boiling water to cover them completely, and let them soak for at least 30 minutes. If you wish to remove the skins, slip them off with your fingers or a small knife, or put the chilies through the finest blade of a food mill.

Canned chilies should always be rinsed in cold water (to remove the brine in which they were preserved) before they are cut and seeded.

VARIETIES OF CHILIES

The mildest chile results from using a mild type of chile that has been ground without seeds and ribs. Always remember that seeds and ribs carry the heat in chile; removing them makes any chile milder. However, in ground chile it is often hard to tell whether it is ground without them. Using chile caribe or grinding chilies yourself is the best way to be sure seeds and ribs are discarded.

Ancho chilies (ahn-cho): These look similar to the bell pepper but are considerably more peppery. They have a firm texture, a bit darker green color when fresh and dark red, almost black when dried.

Jalapeño chilies (hall-la-pay-nyoh): When fresh these chilies have a dark-green, round, firm appearance and are about 2-1/2 inches long and about 1 inch across. They are extremely hot.

Serrano chilies (seh-rrrah-no): These tiny, thin peppers are a deep waxy green, 1 to 1-1/2 inches long, about 1/2 inch thick and are very, very hot. They are rarely available fresh; usually available pickled.

Pequin chilies (peh-keen): These small, oval chilies usually sold dried, often crushed, are referred to as quebrado. They are very hot.

Chile Caribe: Caribe spice is more subtly-flavored and chile made from sun-dried chilies. It can be substituted for chile powder. Most native Southwesterners prefer it, especially for enchiladas.

MOUNTAIN MAN BEANLESS CHILI

7 to 10 pounds of beef brisket or roundsteak
3 medium red onions
1 bottle of beer
5 tablespoons chili powder
5 tablespoons cumin
1 tablespoon sugar
2 tablespoons oregano
2 tablespoons lime juice
2 tablespoons lemon juice
4 tablespoons celery salt
1 tablespoon cayenne pepper
1 tablespoon dry mustard
1 tablespoon dry horseradish
2 tablespoons chicken fat
1 tablespoon paprika
3 tablespoons Worcestershire sauce
3 tablespoons woodruff (hard to find, but worth it)
1 tablespoon crushed red peppers
4 tablespoons Maggi sauce
3 tablespoons Masa Harina
8 finely chopped garlic cloves
6 powdered bay leaves
8 ounces of diced green chilies
2 green bell peppers cut into 1/2" squares
2 red bell peppers cut into 1/2" squares
1 teaspoon tabasco sauce

Trim away all fat and connective tissue from meat. Cut
into bite-sized cubes. Sauté in vegetable oil until well
browned. Pour into a large pot. Chop onions and sauté
in butter or margarine until golden and add to pot along
with the rest of the ingedients. Mix together and add
enough water to make mixture "soupy." Cook over lowest fire about 10 to 16 hours. This should boil down to
proper consistency after all day on the stove. If liquid
goes more quickly, add water as needed. If liquid goes
more slowly, bring temperature up last hour to establish
proper chili consistency at end of slow cook. Let stand
at room temperature for another 12 to 16 hours.

TEXAS CHILI CON CARNE

6 dried ancho chilies, plus 8 dried hot red chilies,
each about 2 inches long
3 cups boiling water
1/2 pound beef suet, preferably kidney suet
3 pounds lean boneless venison or beef chuck
3 medium-sized, finely-crumbled bay leaves
1 tablespoon cumin seeds
2 tablespoons coarsely chopped garlic
4 teaspoons dried oregano
3 tablespoons paprika
1 tablespoon sugar
1 tablespoon salt
3 tablespoons yellow cornmeal

Under cold running water, pull the stems off the ancho and red chilies. Tear chilies in half and brush out their seeds. Cut away any large ribs, chop coarsely, drop them into a bowl, and pour in boiling water. Soak for at least 30 minutes, then strain and reserve liquid. In a heavy 5 to 6-quart casserole, cook the beef suet over moderate heat until it has rendered its fat. Remove and discard the suet bits. Leave about 1/4 cup fat in pot.

Trim fat from meat, cube and cook over moderate heat until firm but not brown. Add 2-1/2 cups of the reserved chili-soaking liquid and bring it to a boil over high heat. Add bay leaves and simmer partially covered for 1 hour. Place cumin in ungreased skillet and toast the seeds over low heat for 10 minutes. In a blender, pulverize the seeds, then add the chilies, remaining chili-soaking liquid, the garlic, oregano, paprika, sugar and salt, and blend again at high speed until all of the ingredients are reduced to a smooth pureé.

Add pureé to meat and simmer partially covered for 30 minutes. Then, stirring constantly, slowly pour in the cornmeal and cook over high heat until the chili comes to a boil and thickens slightly. Add ground hot pepper if desired and serve with freshly cooked pinto beans and rice in separate bowl.

BEEF AND PORK CHILI

2 pounds beef chuck pound
1 pork loin
2 large onions, chopped
3 tablespoons margarine or butter
3 tablespoons olive oil
3 cloves garlic, finely chopped
1 to 2 teaspoons salt
3 tablespoons chili powder
1/2 teaspoon oregano
1/2 teaspoon ground cumin
1 cup tomato pureé
1 cup white wine
2 tablespoons sesame seeds
2 tablespoons parsley, finely chopped
18 to 20 pitted or chopped ripe olives
1/2 ounce unsweetened chocolate

Cut beef and pork into 1-1/2 inch cubes, sauté chopped onions in margarine or butter and oil until golden. Add garlic and cook 3 to 4 minutes. Lightly dredge meat with flour, push the onions and garlic to one side of the pan and quickly sear the meat. Add salt, chili powder, oregano, cumin, tomato pureé and wine. Mix well. Cover and simmer for 1-1/2 hours.

Uncover and test. If the meat is not tender, cook another 20 minutes, or until quite tender, then add sesame seeds, chopped parsley, olives and unsweetened chocolate. Stir and simmer another 30 minutes. The chocolate acts as a binder that pulls the flavors together, and is a slight thickener.

Taste before serving and be sure to add salt and chili powder as desired. Serve with crackers or tortillas. Makes about 4 to 6 servings.

PIONEER PEA SOUP

2 cups dried yellow split peas
1 medium onion studded with 2 whole cloves
cold water
2 medium diced red potatoes
6 ounces salt pork
black pepper and salt to taste

Soak peas overnight. Put into Dutch oven in the morning with enough water to cover. Add the onion, potatoes and salt pork. For campfire cooking, dig a hole deeper than the Dutch oven height, and fill partly with hot coals. Lower Dutch oven into hole and cover top with more coals ("between two fires"). Mound dirt around oven and partially over lid and coals. Let it cook throughout the day and by evening you will have a tasty meal. If cooking on a stove, the heat will be more concentrated and simmering time required will be only 2-1/2 to 3 hours.

RED SALMON SOUP

2 cans of red salmon
2 tablespoon of margarine or butter
2 quarts of milk
black pepper to taste

Heat milk in a heavy pot being careful not to scald. Mash salmon and add to heated milk. Add pepper to taste. Serve with dry toast or crackers.

Santa Fe Bob Sez:

In almost every supermarket in the country you'll find little packets of salt pork. Nowadays, they don't sell very quickly and are purchased by the occasional chef who uses salt pork for flavoring beans or soup. In the Old West, salt pork was the mainstay of pioneers and cowboy camps because it was preserved with salt and because it could be used to flavor otherwise bland food. In the late 1840's, some enterprising publishers wrote a booklet telling the prospective pioneer what to take with him to survive the long, arduous trip. Unfortunately, the authors wrote their book without having made the trip themselves. The booklets were bought by thousands of people and much of the information was misleading. One of their recommendations was to pack several hundred pounds of salt pork per person. By the time the wagons made it to their destination, the horses were exhausted from pulling the heavy load and tons of salt pork had to be disposed of.

CHICKEN WITH AVOCADO SOUP

2 cups of cooked chicken or turkey meat
2 cups of cooked rice
4 cups rich chicken broth
1 cup cooked garbanzos
pinch of leaf oregano
1 chopped chipotle pepper
1 sliced avocado
1 cup cubed Monterey Jack or
Muenster cheese

Chop chicken or turkey into bite-sized pieces. Heat broth to boiling and add chicken, garbanzos, chipotle pepper, rice, and oregano. Serve in large individual bowls, and add cheese pieces and avocado just before serving. Serves 4.

CREAM OF TOMATO/POTATO SOUP

2-1/2 cups potatoes, diced
3 cups tomatoes, peeled, seeded, and cubed
2 onions, sliced
1-1/2 teaspoons flour
2 tablespoons lard or vegetable oil
3 green chilies, diced (4 ounce can)
2 tablespoons ground red chili
1/2 cup light cream

Bring potatoes, tomatoes, and onions to a boil in 1 quart of water. Reduce heat to low and simmer for an hour. Mix flour and oil, add green chilies, and stir into potato-tomato mixture. Stir in red chili, blending thoroughly. Simmer for 20 minutes. Add cream and simmer 5 minutes longer. Makes 6 servings.

HOT, HOT CHILI CON CARNE

3 pounds lean ground beef
2 pounds lean round or flank steak
5 tablespoons vegetable oil
5 cups of finely chopped onions
4 cloves finely minced garlic
6 to 8 tablespoons pure chili powder
2 tablespoons oregano
2 teaspoons ground cumin
1 heaping teaspoon crushed red peppers
1 can (10-1/2 oz.) condensed beef broth
2 cans (15 oz.) tomato sauce
1 can (12 oz.) tomato paste
1 heaping tablespoon salt
1 teaspoon black pepper
1 or 2 tablespoons cornmeal or masa flour (optional)
pound small dry red kidney beans (optional)
pinto beans)
1 cup of beer as thinner when needed

Soak washed beans overnight in 1-1/2 quarts water with a pinch of salt. Cook slowly next day, 2 to 3 hours, until tender. Add water if they cook down.

Heat oil in large heavy iron pot, add onions, and simmer 30 minutes until golden. Add meat gradually, searing and turning constantly until meat starts to brown. Add garlic, beef broth, tomato sauce and paste. Stir well until blended. Slowly add chili powder and other seasonings. Mix well, stirring thoroughly. Cover, and cook at lowest heat for 3 to 4 hours.

Add cooked beans, stir well and let cool. Allow to age in the refrigerator for 12 hours (you can skim the fat off the top) then reheat and serve. Makes about 1 gallon. Serves 8 to 10.

POSOLE

Posole is a Christmas Eve favorite in Mexico, and in New Mexico Posole holds the position that chili holds in Texas. The flavors and textures of cooked meat, corn and raw vegetables in this dish are more subtle and delicate.

4 fresh chile pods made into a paste
3 pig's feet (have butcher cut into quarters)
1 whole head garlic
1 large onion, chopped
3-1/2 to 4 pound chicken
1 pound. lean boneless pork loin
2 cups canned hominy (or an equal amount of fresh or frozen posole)
salt and freshly milled pepper
chicken broth
chile pequins, crumbled
2 limes, cut into wedges
1 bunch radishes
1 head iceberg lettuce, shredded
1 Bermuda onion, minced

First, make chile paste. Open pods, remove stems and seeds, toast on a grill or under boiler for a few minutes until they begin to soften. Then cover with boiling water and soak for 10 minutes. Now puree into a paste. Hotness depends on the kind of peppers you use. Separate garlic into cloves, peel but do not press.

In a soup pot, simmer pig's feet with garlic and onion in salted water for about 3 hours. Cut chicken into serving-sized pieces and chop pork into 2″ cubes. Add chicken and pork and chile paste and cook gently for 45 minutes; add hominy (or posole) and cook 15 more minutes—or until meats are fork-tender. Season to taste with salt and pepper. Skim off excess grease.

If your stock boils down, add chicken broth. Serve in deep soup bowls. Pass bowls of crumbled chilies, limes, radishes, lettuce, and onion, and let everyone garnish soup according to individual tastes. Serves 12.

BLACK BEAN SOUP

1/2 cup olive oil
1/2 pound salt pork or bacon, diced
1/2 pound Westphalian or Black Forest ham, diced
OR 1 pound meaty ham hocks, cut into 2-inch pieces
8 large onions, chopped
8 cloves garlic, minced or pressed
6 large stalks celery (including leaves, if any), chopped
2 pounds (about 5 cups) dried black beans
1/2 teaspoon ground red pepper (cayenne)
4 teaspoons ground cumin
4 large cans (50 oz. each) regular-strength chicken broth
1/4 cup wine vinegar
1 cup dry sherry

Heat oil in a 12-quart pan over medium-high heat. Add salt pork, ham, onions, garlic, and celery. Cook, stirring occasionally, until vegetables are very soft and lightly browned (about 40 minutes).

Remove any debris from beans. Rinse well, drain, and add to pan along with red pepper, cumin, and broth. Bring to a boil over high heat; reduce heat, cover, and simmer until beans mash easily (2-1/2 to 3 hours.) If using ham hocks, lift out and let cool. Remove meat from bones, shred and return to broth. Skim fat from soup and discard.

Blend soup, a little at a time, in a food processor or blender until smooth. Return soup to pan and heat until steaming, stirring often. Blend in vinegar and sherry.

Pass condiments at the table to add to individual servings. Makes 20 servings.

CONDIMENT SUGGESTIONS: Serve a variety of condiments in separate bowls according to your taste: 1/2 inch thick slices of Polish sausage, hot cooked rice, thinly sliced radishes, chopped hard-boiled eggs, sweet pickle spears, diced green, yellow and red bell peppers and olives.

PORK & WHITE BEANS
WITH GREEN CHILI

2 large green bell peppers, seeded
3 tablespoons vegetable oil
2 cups sliced green onions (including tops)
8 cloves garlic, minced or pressed
4 teaspoons ground cumin
6 cans (13 oz. each) tomatillos
4 cans (7 oz. each) diced green chilies
6 cans (15 oz. each) Italian white beans
or 9 cups cooked small white beans
3 pounds boneless pork shoulder or butt
4 teaspoons dry oregano leaves
1/2 teaspoon cayenne pepper
1/2 cup lightly packed fresh cilantro leaves

Thinly slice bell peppers crosswise. Heat oil in a 12-quart pan over medium-high heat. Add bell peppers, onions, garlic, and cumin. Cook, stirring occasionally, until onions are soft (about 5 minutes). Mix in tomatillos (break up with a spoon) and their liquid, chilies, beans, pork, oregano, and red pepper.

Bring to a boil. Reduce heat and simmer until pork is tender when pierced (1-1/2 to 2 hours). For a thinner consistency cook covered. If you prefer a thicker dish, cook uncovered. Stir occasionally. Set aside a few cilantro leaves and chop remaining leaves. Stir in chopped cilantro and use reserved leaves for a garnish. Makes 10 to 12 servings.

PUEBLO LAMB STEW

1 pound dried pinto beans
2 pounds large lamb shanks
1 large chopped onion
3 cloves of minced or pressed garlic
1 tablespoon coriander seeds, crushed
1/2 teaspoon coarsely ground pepper
6 cups water
Salt
2 to 3 medium-size chopped tomatoes
1 cup chopped green onions (including tops)

Sort beans to remove any debris from beans. Rinse well and drain. In a 5-quart pan, combine beans, lamb, onion, garlic, coriander seeds, pepper, and water. Bring to a boil over high heat; then reduce heat, cover, and simmer until beans are tender (1-1/2 to 2 hours), stirring occasionally.

Remove lamb from pan. Cut away bones and fat then cut into bite-sized pieces and return to pan. Skim fat from broth, then season stew to taste with salt.

Serve stew in deep bowls and pass tomatoes and green onions in separate bowls to add to each serving. Makes 6 servings.

COLD AVOCADO SOUP

1 tablespoon vegetable oil
1 clove garlic, minced or pressed
1/2 cup chopped onion
3 large ripe avocados
1/4 cup lemon juice
3 tablespoons dry sherry
1 tablespoon chicken bullion
2-1/2 cups hot water
3/4 teaspoon liquid hot pepper seasoning
2 tablespoons chopped fresh cilantro
2 cups milk
salt

In a small pan heat oil over medium heat. Add garlic and onion; cook, stirring often, until onion is soft (about 10 minutes). Set aside to cool.

Pit and peel and slice 2 of the avocados. Mix in a blender along with lemon juice, onion mixture, and sherry. Continue to blend until pureed. In a bowl, mix bullion with hot water until dissolved. Add to avocado mixture along with hot pepper seasoning, then blend until smoothly pureed. Pour pureé into a bowl and stir in cilantro, and milk. Season to taste with salt. Cover and refrigerate for at least 4 hours or until next day.

Pit, peel, and slice remaining avocado. Ladle soup into mugs and top with avocado. Serve with a small bowl of salted pumpkin seeds to add interest. Makes 6 servings.

BUFFALO KETTLE

Lean, flavorful buffalo meat is available in supermarkets more often than you might expect. It's typically sold as ground meat patties, often in the freezer case. Ask your butcher about it.

2 large onions, chopped
2 tablespoons olive oil or vegetable oil
3/4 pound mushrooms, thinly sliced
1 pound ground buffalo or ground sirloin
2 cans (13 ounces each) tomatillos
1 can (15-1/2 ounces) hominy, drained
1 can (15 ounces) baby corn, drained
1/4 cup chopped fresh cilantro
1 tablespoon dry oregano leaves
5 small dried hot red chilies

In a 5 to 6 quart pan over medium heat, combine onions and 1 tablespoon of the oil; stir often until onions are light golden and sweet to taste (about 20 minutes). Add mushrooms and stir occasionally until liquid evaporates (about 10 more minutes). Pour mixture out of pan; set aside.

Add remaining tablespoon of oil to pan along with buffalo meat. Stir frequently over high heat until meat is well browned and crumbly (about 10 minutes).

Return onion mixture to pan along with tomatillos (break up with a spoon) and their liquid. Stir to free browned bits from bottom of pan. Add hominy, corn, cilantro, oregano, and chilies. Bring to a boil. Reduce heat, cover, and simmer for about 15 minutes, stirring occasionally to blend flavors. Spoon out and discard hot chilies before serving, if desired. Serve with warm soft tortillas and a crisp green salad. Makes 4 to 6 servings.

TEX-MEX CHILI

cooked pinto beans (recipe follows)
4 ounces dried red New Mexico or California chilies
2 cans (12 oz. each) beer
8 pounds bone-in beef chuck
2 tablespoons vegetable oil
4 large onions, chopped
1 head garlic (about 15 cloves), minced or pressed
1-1/2 tablespoons each chili powder and paprika
4 teaspoons ground cumin
1 tablespoon dry oregano leaves
1-1/2 teaspoons sugar
1 teaspoon ground coriander
1/2 teaspoon cayenne pepper
1/4 teaspoon ground allspice
1 can (14-1/2 ounces) regular-strength chicken broth
1 can (8 oz.) tomato sauce
2 tablespoons bourbon whiskey (optional)
salt

Soak pinto beans overnight, then cook as as in follow-ing recipe. Rinse chilies and discard stems and seeds. Break chilies into pieces and combine with beer in a 5-quart pan. Bring to a boil over high heat; then reduce heat, cover, and simmer until chilies are soft (about 30 minutes). Pureé chilies and their cooking liquid in a food processor or blender. With a spoon, push puree through a fine wire strainer and discard residue. Set puree aside.

Cut beef from bones. Trim and discard excess fat; cut meat into 1-inch cubes. Heat oil in a 10-quart pan over medium-high heat. Add meat, a little at a time, and cook until well browned on all sides. Lift out meat and set aside.

Add onions and garlic to pan. Cook over medium heat, stirring often, until onions are soft (about 10 minutes). Add chili powder, paprika, cumin, oregano, sugar, coriander, red pepper, and allspice. Cook, stirring, for 2 minutes. Add beef and any juices that have accumulated, chile puree, broth, tomato sauce, and whiskey, if used. Stir well, then bring to a boil over high heat; reduce heat, cover, and simmer, stirring occasionally, until beef is very tender (about 2 hours). Season to taste with salt. Serve chili in individual bowls and top with beans and condiments. The flavor of this exceptional chili really benefits from a day or two in the refrigerator. Just reheat and serve. Makes 10 to 12 servings.

COOKED PINTO BEANS

Sort 1 pound of dried pinto beans and remove any debris. Rinse beans and place in a large bowl; cover with water and let stand until next day.

Drain beans, discarding liquid. Combine beans, 8 cups water, and 1 dry bay leaf in a 5-quart pan. Bring to a boil over high heat. Reduce heat, cover, and simmer until beans are very tender (1 to 11/2 hours). Season to taste with salt. Drain beans before serving.

CONDIMENT SUGGESTIONS

Serve in separate bowls: shredded Cheddar or Jack cheese, sour cream, diced tomatoes, sliced green onions (including tops), ripe olives, sliced ripe avocados and tortilla chips according to your taste.

BAKED COUNTRY ONION SOUP

1/2 cup butter or margarine
1/4 cup vegetable oil
5 large onions, thinly sliced
1 quart chicken broth
1 quart beef bouillon broth
1/8 teaspoon ground black pepper
1/2 cup white wine
6 slices toasted garlic bread
shredded monterey Jack cheese

In a soup kettle or Dutch oven melt butter or margarine and blend in vegetable oil. Sauté onions 3-5 minutes. Reduce heat and cook, stirring occasionally, for one hour. Add chicken broth, beef bouillon broth, pepper and wine. Bring mixture to a boil. Then reduce heat and simmer on low for 30 minutes.

Pour soup into six oven-proof soup bowls. Float a slice of garlic bread on top of each bowl. Sprinkle shredded cheese over tops. Bake in hot (400° F.) oven until cheese melts and lightly browns.

OYSTER SOUP

oysters, two 8-ounce cans
oyster crackers
1 tablespoon of butter,or margarine
2 cups of milk
1 cup of light or heavy cream
a pinch of ground mace
a pinch of ground nutmeg
a pinch ground pepper

Drain liquid from oysters into measuring cup and add water to make 1 cup liquid. Heat this liquid in saucepan or kettle with another cup of water. Crush enough oyster crackers to produce 2 cup of fine crumbs, and stir them, along with butter, into hot liquid. When boiling starts, add oysters and simmer 1 to 2 minutes.

Add milk, cream, mace, nutmeg, and pepper, and return just to boil. Remove from heat and ladle into bowls. Serve with side dish of oyster crackers. Makes six small servings.

CHUCK WAGON BEEF SOUP

1-1/2 pounds flank steak
4 tablespoons of flour
1-1/2 teaspoons of salt
2 twists ground black pepper
3 tablespoons vegetable oil
1 can whole kernel corn.
1 can red beans
2 cups chicken broth
1-1/2 cups of water
1 clove garlic, minced
1-1/2 teaspoons of chili powder
1/2 teaspoon of hot pepper sauce
3 small onions, chopped
1/2 cup green pepper, chopped

Cut flank steak into 1/2" cubes. Combine flour, salt and pepper and dredge beef pieces. Brown beef in oil in kettle or Dutch oven. Drain drippings. Add corn and bean liquid, but reserve corn and beans until later. Also add chicken broth, water, garlic and chili powder. Cover and cook over low heat for about two hours. Add onions and green pepper and cook another 20 minutes. Add corn and beans and simmer 10 minutes. Serve with hot cornbread.

OLD-TIME BEEF-VEGETABLE SOUP

2 pounds beef short ribs
1/2 cup flour
1 teaspoons salt
4 tablespoons of vegetable oil
3 quarts of water
1 teaspoon of paprika
black peppercorns
1 bay leaf
3 sprigs fresh parsley
2 chopped onions
4 stalks chopped celery
3 sliced carrots
3 ripe tomatoes, peeled and quartered
1 potato, peeled and diced
1 cup whole kernel corn
1 teaspoon Worcestershire sauce

Dredge ribs in flour mixed with salt. Heat oil in skillet and brown meat. Place browned meat in a soup kettle with water, paprika, peppercorns, bay leaf and parsley. Bring to a boil and skim fat from surface. Cover and let simmer for 2-1/2 hours. Lift ribs from kettle, let cool and remove meat. Discard fat and bones. Chop up meat into bite-sized pieces and return to kettle. Add vegetables and Worcestershire sauce. Continue cooking over low heat until vegetables are tender. Serve in deep bowls with freshly made warm, sourdough bread.

COWBOY STEW
WITH DUMPLINGS

2 pounds lean bacon
carrots
onions
cabbage
potatoes
turnips

Cut bacon in small squares and boil until about half done. Then add chopped vegetables. Season to taste. When almost done add dumplings as follows.

Rawhide Dumplings
2 cups flour
1/2 teaspoon salt
cold water

Sift flour and salt, add water to make stiff dough. Roll paper thin. Cut into squares. Drop into boiling stew and cook an additional 12 minutes. These dumplings are also good in chicken broth or beans that are quite soupy. The secret of making them is to roll them very thin.

STEWED LAMB WITH OYSTERS

Cut about 2 pounds of nice lamb (a breast piece, if possible) into one inch squares. Season with sage, parsley, salt, and a dash of cayenne. Stew in just enough water to cover, until tender. Add a cupful of cream, and when it boils, add 2 dozen fresh oysters. Serve as soon as the oysters begin to curl.

Game Meats

Historically, human beings have lived primarily by hunting. Our distant ancestors gathered roots, grains and berries whenever they could, but they lived largely on wild game. They had the best of reasons: game was available all year. As civilization progressed and human populations increased, game became less plentiful. By the early Middle Ages, all hunting in Europe was reserved exclusively for the aristocracy.

Then a new world, America, was discovered. In this land game once again was cheap and abundant for everyone. Here there were no restrictions, no preserves. Wildlife in colonial times was regarded as a nuisance to be slaughtered as rapidly as possible. During the mid-eighteen hundreds when the transcontinental railroads were built, buffalo, antelope, elk, and bighorn sheep were killed by professional hunters to feed the workmen.

For city folk, market hunters provided prairie chicken, venison, passenger pigeons, railbirds, wild duck, buffalo and other game for people who lived in the cities. Prices were low. At one time you could buy a 20-pound turkey for fifty cents or an entire deer for a dollar.

As America became civilized, the cattle and sheep raised in the Old West became commonly available as food. Game consequently became less important to the human diet.

By the end of the nineteenth century, hunting and shrinking habitat wiped out game in many areas. World

Today game is again available and abundant game populations are thriving thanks to regulated hunting.

Old West game recipes are simple enough so that the interesting, special taste of game comes through. Wine was used in recipes to keep the game moist and to enhance the flavor. If you prefer, substitute chicken broth or apple cider for white wine and beef broth for red wine. Cooks generally didn't drown a pheasant in so much cream sauce it tasted exactly like chicken, or prepare delicious venison to make it indistinguishable from veal or beef. Game meals were both tasty and enjoyable, and provided a welcome change from the everyday fare of the pioneer.

OVEN-BARBECUED RIBS

10 pounds of deer
mountain sheep, or elk ribs
1/2 cup sorghum molasses
1/2 teaspoon dry mustard
1/2 cup white wine vinegar
1/2 teaspoon course ground pepper
1 teaspoon paprika
2 teaspoons salt

Mix the sorghum, mustard, vinegar, pepper, paprika, and salt. Using a brush, coat the ribs with this mixture. Coat oven rack with Pam or other oil to prevent meat from sticking. Preheat oven to 475°F. Place ribs on rack over a large, shallow pan of water to catch the drippings.

Turn from time to time and spread with more of the sauce. Cook until the edges show crisp and the coating is brown. Serves 10 to 15.

BAKED POSSUM

Bring a large kettle of water to a boil. Then remove kettle from fire. Drop the unskinned possum into the water until the surface hair can be easily pulled out. Remove possum from kettle and skin.

Clean and cut into serving pieces. Roll pieces in flour seasoned with salt, pepper, and garlic. Melt 1/4 cup butter or margarine in a heavy iron skillet and brown meat pieces.

Slice vegetables (onions, carrots, celery, potatoes) over meat pieces. Pour a cup of sour cream over the skillet contents. Cover skillet and bake in a 300°F. oven for approximately 1-1/2 hours.

PHEASANT IN CREAM SAUCE

1 pheasant, quartered
salt
1 can condensed cream of mushroom soup
1/2 cup sour cream
3/4 cups fresh, sliced mushrooms
1/4 cup grated Parmesan cheese
1/4 cup onion, chopped

Preheat oven to 350°F. Rub pheasant quarters with salt and place them in baking dish with skin side up. In separate bowl mix together the mushroom soup, sour cream, mushrooms, cheese and onion.

Spread this mixture over the pheasant and bake in oven for 1-1/2 to 2 hours or until tender. Baste occasionally with sauce during baking. Serve with wild rice on the side. Serves 3 to 4

SQUIRREL PIE

1 8-inch pie shell, unbaked
2 tablespoons fresh parsley, chopped
2 squirrels, skinned and cleaned
flour
1 teaspoon salt
1/8 teaspoon pepper
dash of tabasco sauce
3 tablespoons butter or margarine
1 onion, chopped

Cut meat into serving pieces and place in a kettle or large saucepan and just cover with water. Add a teaspoon of salt and pepper.

Cover kettle and cook over low heat until meat is tender. Drain off liquid and set aside. Remove meat from bones. Discard bones. In a large skillet melt butter and lightly fry onions. Stir in parsley. Measure the liquid drained from kettle. For each cup of the reserved liquid add 1-1/2 tablespoons of flour to skillet mixture. Add a tablespoon at a time and mix well. Add the reserved liquid slowly, stirring constantly. Bring to a boil. Add tabasco sauce. Drop meat pieces into boiling mixture. Pour entire mixture into pie shell and bake in 425°F. oven for 15 minutes.

STEWED JACK RABBIT AND DUMPLINGS

If you can't find a hunter to give you a skinned rabbit (he will want the pelt), look for a farm-raised rabbit at a local butcher shop or look for fresh or frozen rabbit at the supermarket. Your stew will be all white meat.

> *3 pound rabbit, dressed, with giblets*
> *6 ounces salt pork*
> *2 tablespoons flour*
> *Dumplings (recipe follows)*

Cut the rabbit into eight serving pieces (two forelegs, two rib sections, two backs, and two hind legs). Simmer giblets in saucepan with 2 cups of water. Slice salt pork and dice it with a chopper. Brown the diced pieces in a Dutch oven or casserole over medium heat; remove the pieces and save.

Brown the rabbit pieces in the pork fat in the Dutch oven, taking care to avoid spattering fat. This will take 10 to 15 minutes. Add the giblet liquid; cover and simmer for 35 to 40 minutes.

Meanwhile prepare gravy thickening. In a heavy skillet, over medium heat, toast the flour until it resembles cocoa powder, stirring constantly to prevent burning. This will take 10 to 15 minutes. Let flour cool in skillet.

Remove giblets from saucepan and finely chop. Return them to saucepan, add browned flour, and work into a paste. Slowly blend in 1 cup of water.

As the stew continues to simmer, prepare dumpling dough according to following recipe.

When the meat is just tender, stir in cooked, diced salt pork and sauce-pan gravy into the Dutch oven. With a soupspoon, drop the dumpling dough onto the bubbling liquid, covering the surface. Let simmer on medium-low heat until dumplings puff and lose their gloss (about 10 minutes). Cover with a lid, reduce heat to low, and simmer another 10 minutes, until dumplings are cooked through.

Serve with cornbread and molasses. Serves 6.

DUMPLINGS

This recipe will produce enough dumplings to complete the Jack Rabbit Stew and can be used for a variety of your own recipes.

> *2 cups flour*
> *1 heaping teaspoon salt*
> *1 teaspoon baking soda*
> *3/4 to 1 cup cultured buttermilk*

In a large bowl, mix dry ingredients well. Pour in 3/4 cup of the buttermilk and mix quickly with a fork. The dough should be stiff but too moist for rolling. Add remaining milk if needed.

Be sure your stew or broth is simmering on the stove. With a soupspoon drop the dough onto the bubbling liquid, covering the surface. Let simmer on medium-low heat until dumplings puff and lose their gloss (8 to 10 minutes). Cover with a lid, reduce heat to low, and simmer another 8 to 10 minutes, until dumplings are cooked through. Dumplings in a skillet can be cooked uncovered by turning them halfway through.

Santa Fe Bob sez:

Here's a little hint from a pioneer hunter who wanted to be sure to bring home a pheasant or duck for dinner. Soak wheat in strong alcohol. Scatter it where the birds are in the habit of feeding. Take them while they are drunk!

The sanitation, refrigeration and modern kitchens of today allow meat storage with no spoilage. However, the modern hunter always follows this rule: Kill it quickly, clean it at once, and cool it as rapidly as possible.

Cleaning the game birds, waterfowl and small animals that were abundant in the Old West wasn't much trouble. Big game such as deer or big-horned sheep were a little more difficult. That "gamey flavor" associated with wild meats was a taste preferred by people of the Old West. It was the result of the way game was cared for in the field and the way it was "hung" to cure, which was the way that pioneer hunters allowed their meat to decompose slightly in order to make it more tender. Nowadays, dressing and freezing game meats does the same thing with no risk of tainting.

CHILI VENISON

2 pounds venison meat, cut into l-inch cubes
flour
1/4 cup lard or vegetable shortening
1 large onion, chopped
2 cloves garlic, peeled and minced
2 4-ounce cans of green chili peppers, sliced
4 medium-sized green tomatoes, cubed
1 teaspoon salt
1 teaspoon cumin
1/2 teaspoon oregano

Dredge venison in flour. In a large, heavy saucepan, sauté meat in lard or other shortening until lightly browned. Transfer to a plate.

Sauté onion, garlic, and chili peppers in same pan until onion is slightly wilted.

Return meat to pan with remaining ingredients. Add enough water to cover and simmer for 2-3 hours or until tender. Makes 6 servings

PUEBLO VENISON STEW

2 pounds venison, cut into 1-inch cubes
flour
1/4 cup lard or vegetable oil
1 large onion, chopped
2 cloves garlic, peeled and minced
1 medium-sized sweet green pepper, chopped
1 cup dry corn kernels
1 cup dry pinto beans
1/2 cup pinon nuts, chopped
1/4 cup sunflower seeds, shelled and crushed
2 dried juniper berries, crushed
salt and pepper to taste

Dredge venison in flour. In a large, heavy saucepan, sauté venison until lightly browned. Transfer to a plate. Sauté onion, garlic and pepper in same pan until onion is slightly wilted.

Return meat to pan with remaining ingredients. Add enough water to cover venison and vegetables. Simmer for 3 hours or until tender. Makes 6 servings.

ROAST GOOSE WITH PEAR STUFFING

1 goose, 7-12 pounds. (a 7-pound. goose serves 6)
2 apples, halved
2 stalks celery, quartered
2 onions, quartered
salt and coarsely ground pepper

Preheat oven to 350°F. Wash goose and wipe dry. Rub inside cavity with salt. Place 1/2 apple, 1 stalk of celery, and 1 quartered onion in the wishbone or neck cavity. Skewer the neck skin to the back and fold the wings behind the back. Stuff the rear cavity with remaining apple, celery, and onion. Skewer the cavity shut. Salt and pepper the goose generously and place on a rack inside a roasting pan with a lid. The rack is needed so that the goose will not fry in the accumulated grease. Cover pan tightly and roast 3 to 5 hours or until the leg joint moves freely. If the level of grease creeps up to touch the bird, remove it with a bulb baster. Uncover pan the last 30 minutes to complete browning. Remove stuffing. You should allow the bird to stand 20 minutes before carving. Save the legs for leftovers and cut the breast into paper-thin slices, each bordered by a strip of crisp skin.

The stuffing which is served with the bird is cooked in a separate pan during the 30 minutes the goose is browning. The quality of the stuffing will be determined largely by the bread you use. A firm homemade or sourdough bread is recommended.

PEAR STUFFING

2 cups dried pears, stewed
2 quarts white bread, cubed
1/2 cup diced onion
3/4 cup butter
2 cups chicken broth
1 tablespoon salt
1/4 teaspoon coarsely ground pepper

1 teaspoon poultry seasoning
1 6-1 /2 ounce can salted cashew nuts

Stew pears in a small amount of water until soft, then dice fine. Meanwhile cut bread into small cubes. Sauté onion in butter, mix with the bread, and toast mixture in the oven until dry. Moisten with the broth, add seasonings, pears, and cashews, place in bread pan, and bake for 30 minutes at 350°F. This is so good the second day, you can make it a day ahead and reheat it with fine results. Whatever you do, mix with a light touch so you don't smash the bread cubes. Heavy mixing results in soggy, brick-like stuffing.

GIBLET GRAVY

giblets and neck of goose
2 cups water
salt and pepper to taste
2 tablespoons cornstarch
1/4 cup water

While the goose is roasting, place the giblets and neck in a small pan and cover with 2 cups of water. Salt and pepper to taste. Simmer 3 hours, adding water as necessary. Just before you're ready to serve the dinner, strain sauce into a second pan, cut giblets fine, and add them to the sauce. Discard the neck. Bring sauce to a rolling boil and add the cornstarch moistened in water. Taste again and season to suit. Cook and stir until you have a clear, thick gravy.

QUAIL IN WINE SAUCE

This is a good basic game bird recipe that is good for just about any variety of bird.

6 quail
1 bay leaf
1 teaspoon chives
1/2 teaspoon salt
2 whole cloves
1/4 teaspoon pepper
1 teaspoon peppercorns
1/2 cup cooking oil
2 cups dry white wine
2 cloves garlic, pressed
2 medium onions, minced
pinch cayenne pepper
1 pint heavy cream

In a stew pot cook the onions in oil until clear, with cloves, peppercorns, garlic, and bay leaf. Add quail and brown on all sides. Add wine, salt, pepper, cayenne pepper, and chives. Simmer with a lid on the pot until tender (from 45 minutes to 1-1/2 hours).

Remove quail to hot serving dish. Strain sauce. Place sauce in saucepan and boil, reducing by half. Now add heavy cream and stir. Season to taste. Heat to boiling and pour over quail.

This makes a thin sauce. If you prefer more of a gravy, thicken sauce with 1 tablespoon of cornstarch dissolved in 1/2 cup cold water. Pour in a thin stream into hot cream. Cook and stir until sauce becomes thick and translucent. Serve with wild rice on the side. Serves 6.

Santa Fe Bob sez:

If you are ever associated with a hunter, you will discover this interesting quirk: The hunter will want you to make use of the game. All of it. Here is a recipe for paté that's a delicious way to utilize game meat.

TEXAS PATÉ

1/2 deer liver (or 1 goat kid liver), roughly 3 pounds
3 eggs
1/4 pound bacon
2 onions, chopped
1 fresh jalapeño, chopped
1/2 teaspoon salt
1 teaspoon coarse ground pepper
2 slices bread

Cut the liver into thin slices. Cut out any blood vessels and discard. Broil liver, 2 minutes on each side. Once the liver is broiled, wash and dry. Hard-boil the eggs. Now fry the bacon. Remove bacon and sauté the onions in the bacon grease. While onions are sautéing, run the liver through the food grinder, using a coarse blade. Now place the chopped liver in the bacon grease with jalapeño and onion mixture. Add salt and pepper to taste. Cook and stir over medium heat for 5 minutes. Peel the eggs. Remove liver, jalapeño, and onions from the grease and run through the grinder two more times, along with the hard-cooked eggs, bacon, and bread. Mix with your hands. Moisten the mixture with some of the bacon grease. Grease a 1-1/2 quart mold lightly with bacon grease, letting excess drip out, press the liver mixture into the mold, and chill. Turn out onto a flat plate and serve with stone-ground crackers.

SESAME-FRIED DOVE

12 doves
1 egg
1/2 cup milk
1 cup flour
1 tablespoon salt
1 tablespoon freshly cracked pepper
4 tablespoons. sesame seeds
oil for deep-frying

Choose only young doves with white skin for frying. Mix egg and milk. Place flour, salt, pepper, and sesame seeds in a brown paper bag. Shake birds in flour, then in egg and milk, then in flour again. Let the birds stand while the oil gets hot so that the batter will set. Deep-fry in oil at 375°F. until golden brown. Serves 4.

TAOS RABBIT

1 medium sized rabbit
2 tablespoons lard or vegetable oil
1 large onion, peeled and diced
2 quarts water
1 cup white wine vinegar
3 teaspoons ground red chili
1 teaspoon salt
1/2 cup cornmeal (blue or yellow)

Cut rabbit into serving pieces. Place in a large saucepan and brown meat in lard or oil.

Add remaining ingredients and simmer, covered, for 1-1/2 hours or until meat is tender.

Add cornmeal gradually to pan, blending thoroughly. Simmer for 10 minutes until sauce thickens. Makes 6 servings.

VENISON STEAK

1 venison round steak, 1-inch thick
flour
1 teaspoon ground red chili
salt to taste
1 medium-sized onion, chopped
2 teaspoons lard or vegetable shortening
3 small tomatoes
3 dried juniper berries, crushed

Dust steak with flour, ground chili and salt. In a large heavy skillet, sauté onion in lard or shortening until slightly wilted.

Add tomatoes and berries and enough water to cover. Simmer for 50 minutes or until tender.

Beef may be substituted for venison. Makes 4 servings.

Salads

If you take the time to look at a map of the Old West you will notice that a good portion of it is actually a desert. The only thing pioneers and camp cooks had to start with in the way of salad greens was weeds. On the frontier, gardens were sparse and short-lived. Obviously, times have changed. Good fresh fruits and vegetables are available on a year-round basis even in the smallest of towns. There is a revival of interest in home gardens. But the tradition of salad making in the Old West is scant.

Salads are relatively recent additions to Western meals and are largely due to the inspired creativity of contemporary cooks especially in California where a huge variety of produce readily cultivated. There, avocados, lettuce, cheese, tomatoes, olives, various meat-laden sauces and beans or other hearty vegetables have been combined with the greatest of ease, resulting in colorful main-dish salads. Traditionally salads of the Old West were marinated or pickled vegetables or fruit salads, and were never served as a main course.

In frontier times, salad most likely showed up as a garnish like lettuce, tomatoes and other fresh vegetables to accompany other dishes.

For that reason, the salad needs the attention of the contemporary cook in order to make it an integral part of the meal. In the first place, never cut any kind of lettuce. Lettuce torn into bite-sized chunks looks lively and has a pleasant, fluffy texture. In the second place, unappetizing bottled dressing can ruin a beautiful salad. Anyone who spends hours preparing a wonderful meal should be careful not to spoil the enjoyment. A harsh vinegar and corn oil salad dressing or too much dressing destroys the taste of the fresh salad ingredients. The palate is also numbed, so that after the salad, who cares what comes next? A well-made green salad should be topped with a subtle, carefully blended dressing that will make people so hungry they'll be eagerly anticipating the rest of the dinner.

Since traditional salads are in short supply, you should try inventing salads by reversing the usual presentation of certain vegetables. Experiment with raw squash or cooked lettuce. It can be interesting to transpose in the vegetable department. Use your own creativity to come up with salads to accompany foods from the Old West.

ASPARAGUS WITH TOMATILLOS

1 pound asparagus
3 tablespoons olive oil
4 large tomatillos (about 1-1/2-inch in diameter)
1 small Roma-type tomato
1/4 cup finely shredded Parmesan cheese
lemon wedges
salt and pepper

Husk, core and finely dice tomatillos. Core and finely dice Roma tomato. Cut off and discard tough ends of asparagus; rinse spears well. In a deep, wide frying pan, bring about 1 inch water to a boil over high heat; add asparagus and cook, uncovered, until barely tender when pierced (3 to 5 minutes). Drain and immerse in ice water. When cool, drain again; then arrange equally on 4 salad plates or arrange all asparagus on a serving platter.

In a bowl, mix oil, tomatillos, and tomato; evenly spoon over asparagus. Sprinkle with cheese. Garnish with lemon wedges. Season to taste with salt and pepper. Makes 4 servings.

CHILE COLESLAW

1 large head of cabbage
1 mild fresh chile
1 medium onion
1/2 cup each white wine vinegar and water
olive or vegetable oil
sugar, to taste
2 tablespoons olive oil or vegetable oil

Shred cabbage. Chop chile (remove stems and seeds) and onion very fine. Add to cabbage and salt to taste. Mix vinegar and water, sweetened to taste, and stir in well with small amount olive or cooking oil. Pour over cabbage mixture and refrigerate for an hour before serving.

GINGER ALE SALAD

1 tablespoon vegetable oil
1 small Temple or Navel orange
1/2 cup cold water
1 envelope unfavored gelatin
1/4 cup sugar
1-1/2 cups ginger ale
2 tablespoons strained fresh lemon juice
2 medium-sized firm ripe peaches
1/2 cup fresh ripe strawberries
1/2 cup table grapes, washed, halved and seeded
1 tablespoon very finely chopped crystallized ginger

With a pastry brush, spread the vegetable oil evenly inside a 1-quart decorative mold. Invert the mold on paper towels to drain off the excess oil.

Peel, halve, pitt or husk peaches and strawberries and cut lengthwise into 1/3 inch-thick slices.

Remove the peel and all of the white membrane of the orange with a small sharp knife, using short sawing motions. Section the orange by cutting along both sides of each membrane division to the core. As each section is freed, carefully lift it out and set it aside on paper towels to drain.

Pour the water into a heatproof measuring cup and sprinkle the gelatin over it. When the gelatin has softened for 2 or 3 minutes, set the cup in a small skillet of simmering water and stir over low heat until the gelatin dissolves completely. Add the sugar and stir until it dissolves.

Pour the gelatin mixture into a deep bowl and stir in the ginger ale and lemon juice. Then set the bowl into a larger bowl half filled with crushed ice or ice cubes and cold water. With a metal spoon, stir the mixture until it thickens enough to flow sluggishly off the spoon. Stir in the orange sections, peaches, strawberries, grapes and the crystallized ginger.

Pour the mixture into the oiled mold, cover with foil or plastic wrap, and refrigerate for at least 4 hours, or until it is firm to the touch.

To unmold the salad, run a thin knife around the sides of the mold and dip the bottom briefly into hot water. Place an inverted serving plate on top of the mold and, grasping plate and mold together firmly, turn them over.

Rap the plate on a table and the ginger-ale salad should slide out easily. Refrigerate until ready to serve.

Garnish plate with cucumber slices, watercress and strawberry halves. Serve with poppy-seed or strawberry sour cream dressing (see recipes at the end of this chapter. Makes 6 to 8 servings.

HOT CHILE POTATO SALAD

6 to 8 red potatoes
1/2 cup each finely chopped chilies, carrots,
onions, pickles, and celery
salt and butter or margarine, to taste
1/4 cup cider vinegar
1/4 cup sour cream
4 hard-boiled eggs, chopped

Boil and dice potatoes. Season with butter or margarine and salt to taste. Add the rest of the vegetables. Stir in vinegar and add chopped eggs. Serve warm.

CHILE COTTAGE CHEESE

1 cup cottage cheese
1/4 cup mayonnaise
1/2 cup finely chopped chilies
1/2 cup finely chopped onion
1/2 cup finely chopped carrots

Combine all ingredients and serve on salad greens. Serves 4 to 6.

CRUSHED PINEAPPLE SALAD

1 package orange gelatin
1 cup hot water
1 cup whipping cream
1 cup sugar
1 small can crushed pineapple
small can white grapes
2 cups raw ground cranberries

Pour 1 cup boiling water over orange gelatin. Mix cranberries with sugar in a bowl and set aside. After gelatin has cooled, whip until light and frothy. Whip cream and combine with gelatin . Add cranberries, pineapple, and grapes. Chill in mold. Turn out on a bed of romaine lettuce arranged on a chilled serving platter.

BEAN SALAD

2 cups cooked pinto beans
2 cups cooked green beans
1 large onion, peeled and sliced thinly
2 cloves garlic, peeled and mashed
1 large sweet pepper, seeded and thinly sliced
1/2 cup sugar
1 teaspoon ground red chili
2 teaspoons salt
1/3 cup vinegar
1/2 cup oil

Combine pinto and green beans, onion, garlic, and pepper in a large bowl.
Combine sugar, chili, salt, and vinegar in another bowl. Slowly pour in oil, beating constantly.
Pour over beans and toss thoroughly. Allow beans to marinate, covered, for at least 2 hours in the refrigerator before serving. Makes 6-8 servings

Santa Fe Bob sez:

Salads were not eaten in the Old West as a part of a balanced meal. They were eaten simply because those particular ingredients happened to be available. The concept of salads to add nutrition, balance, and color had not yet developed in American cuisine. Cooks in Boston and Philadelphia were experimenting with salads after the Civil War. But those cities were more advanced than the western frontier. By the beginning of the 20th century, a few rural households were beginning to eat raw vegetables and "salads." But this was still a new idea for people accustomed to dandelion greens. By late winter the food supplies of many pioneer folk had become moldy and rancid. They eagerly awaited the first green growth of spring!

SAN DIEGO SALAD

Avocados festively accented with oranges, grapes, and jicama and dressed with a tart dressing make an unusual salad that is both beautiful and delicious. Never make it more than 1 hour in advance, although the basic preparation of the fruits can be done ahead.

5 large, ripe Haas or Fuerte avocados
1/4 cup freshly squeezed lime juice
2 heads fluffy leaf lettuce
5 seedless oranges, peeled and sliced in thin rounds
2 jicamas, peeled and coarsely shredded
1 large bunch (about 2 cups) seedless white grapes
Avo Dressing (recipe follows)

Halve and peel the avocados, then slice them into long thin wedges. Sprinkle lime juice over all, carefully stirring to coat each piece evenly.

Arrange the lettuce leaves on chilled plates or in a large bowl, then alternate wedges of avocado with slices of orange. Surround the edge of the salad with shredded jicama. Sprinkle grapes across the top. Prepare the dressing and drizzle over the salad just before serving.

AVO DRESSING

2 ripe Haas or Fuerte avocados
2/3 cup freshly squeezed orange juice
1/2 cup fresh lime juice
2 tablespoons honey
1 teaspoon salt
1/2 teaspoon caribe, or other crushed dried red chile

Place all ingredients in a blender jar and process until smooth. Makes 12 servings.

MARINATED AVOCADO SALAD

A perfect complement to almost any Southwestern menu, this great salad offers just a bit of a twist to the traditional guacamole.

1/4 cup freshly squeezed lime juice
3/4 cup extra virgin olive oil
2 garlic cloves, minced
1 tablespoon caribe (or other crushed dried red chile)
3 ripe Haas or Fuerte avocados
1 head red leaf or Boston lettuce

To make dressing combine the lime juice, olive oil, garlic, and caribe. Cut avocados in half, remove pit and skin. Then cut into 1-inch cubes. Place in a favorite pottery serving bowl or a food storage container and gently toss with the dressing so as not to break up the cubes of avocado.

Rinse lettuce leaves and pat dry. To serve, place a portion of the marinated avocado on two to three lettuce leaves on a chilled plate.

If you make ahead, the avocado should be well sealed against oxidation—either by wrapping tight with plastic wrap, placing it carefully down against the avocados, or by sealing into plastic freezer or food storage containers. It will keep at least a day. Makes 6 to 8 servings

CHICORY GRAPEFRUIT SALAD

1 head of curly chicory
2 large red grapefruit, peeled
6 thin slices of a large round red salad onion
1/2 cup vegetable or olive oil
1/4 cup white wine vinegar
1 tablespoon honey

Using chilled plates, place the chicory leaves on each, artfully topping each with a pinwheel design created from the grapefruit sections, which have been carefully cut from the membrane. Be careful not to allow any white from the skin to remain.

Top each with the separated onion rings. For dressing, combine the oil, wine vinegar, and honey and drizzle over each serving.

CORN SALAD

3 cups cooked fresh or frozen corn kernels
1/2 cup pimento, thinly sliced
1 cup cooked lima beans
3/4 cup chopped onion
1-1/2 cups green pepper, finely chopped
1 teaspoon salt
1 teaspoon ground red chili
1/4 cup vinegar
1/3 cup oil

Combine corn, pimento, lima beans, onion, and green pepper in a large mixing bowl.

Combine salt, chili, and vinegar in another bowl. Slowly pour in oil, beating constantly.

Pour dressing over corn mixture and toss thoroughly. Allow salad to marinate, covered, for at least 2 hours in the refrigerator before serving. Makes 6 servings.

~+~+~+~+~+~+~+~+~+~+~+~+~+~+~+~+~

PICKLED COLESLAW

*Coleslaw, especially the pickled variety, is often served
with Southwestern foods. This particular slaw works
well for campers and picnickers because it keeps very
well without refrigeration.*

1 cup vegetable oil
1 cup white or cider vinegar
1-1/4 to 1-1/2 cups sugar
2 tablespoons celery seeds
lettuce leaves (optional)
3 pounds cabbage, chopped
1 medium-size green pepper, finely chopped
2 medium-size white onions, finely chopped
1 tablespoon salt
1/2 teaspoon freshly ground black pepper

Heat the oil, vinegar, sugar and celery seeds until the
mixture boils and the sugar dissolves. Simmer for a few
minutes.

Combine the chopped vegetables in a large bowl.
Season with the salt and pepper and mix well. Pour hot
dressing over the vegetables and let stand for at least 2
hours before serving. You can chill overnight for the
best flavor. Serve on top of lettuce leaves, if desired.

SOUTHWEST POTATO SALAD

5 large red potatoes
3 eggs
6 slices of bacon, cut up
1/4 pound butter or margarine
4 green onions, chopped
1/2 cup dry white wine
1/2 cup chicken stock
1 teaspoon seasoned salt
1/2 teaspoon freshly ground black pepper
1/4 cup chopped green chile (optional)
1/4 cup chopped pimiento
3 tablespoons chopped parsley
4 to 6 cherry tomatoes

Peel potatoes; cook until tender. Meanwhile, hard-cook eggs and fry bacon until crisp. Cook onion in the bacon drippings until onion is translucent. Drain off excess fat.

When potatoes are done cut them into bite-sized pieces. Add the butter in chunks mixing in so as to coat all the potato pieces evenly while hot.

Add remaining ingredients except 1 tablespoon parsley and cherry tomatoes. Mix well until blended. Serve while still warm, garnished with 1 tablespoon parsley and cherry tomatoes. Makes 8 servings.

TOSTADA SALAD

Cilantro Vinaigrette (recipe follows)
vegetable oil
4 flour tortillas (about 8-inch diameter)
1 pound thinly sliced cold rare roast beef
2 to 4 cups shredded lettuce
2 medium-size tomatoes, thinly sliced
1/2 small red onion, thinly sliced and separated
1/2 cup shredded Jack or cheddar cheese
fresh cilantro sprigs
sliced ripe olives and avocados
sour cream

Prepare Cilantro Vinaigrette and set aside.

In a 10 to 12-inch frying pan, heat 1/2 inch oil over medium-high heat. When oil is hot, add 1 tortilla at a time; cook, turning quickly with 2 spatulas, until bubbly and just golden but still flexible (about 30 seconds). Bend tortilla in half at about a 45° angle as you lift it from oil. Drain on paper towels, leaning tortilla against something sturdy (such as a 28-oz. can) so it holds its shape as it cools.

To assemble each tostada, place a fried tortilla on a plate. Top flat surface with 1/4 of the beef, lettuce, tomatoes, onion, and cheese. Garnish with cilantro sprigs, and olives. Serve with avocados and sour cream. Pass vinaigrette to drizzle over individual servings.

CILANTRO VINAIGRETTE

3/4 cup vegetable oil
1/2 cup red wine vinegar
1 teaspoon dry mustard
1 clove garlic, minced or pressed
1/4 cup chopped fresh cilantro
1/8 teaspoon ground red pepper

Combine all ingredients, stir or shake well. Makes 4 servings.

SALAD DRESSINGS

You will find many uses for the following salad dress-
ings . Spice up your favorite salads with these distinc-
tively flavored recipes. The Chile dressings will add a
robust Southwest flavor. The fruit salad dressings add a
unique taste to just about any combination of fresh fruit.

STRAWBERRY SOUR CREAM
DRESSING

1 10-ounce package frozen sliced strawberries
OR 4 cups of sliced fresh strawberries
1-1/2 cups sour cream
pinch of salt
confectioners' sugar(optional)

If using frozen strawberries, thoroughly defrost in a
large bowl with paper towel on bottom to absorb excess
water. Crush the strawberries slightly with the back of a
large spoon. Add the sour cream and salt, and stir until
the ingredients are thoroughly blended. Taste for sweet-
ness and add confectioners' sugar if desired. Cover with
foil or plastic wrap and refrigerate the dressing for at
least 1 hour before serving. Strawberry Sour Cream
Dressing is a good accompaniment to any fruit salad.

THOUSAND ISLAND CHILE DRESSING

1 cup mayonnaise
1/2 cup finely chopped chilies OR 1/3 cup chile sauce
2 tablespoons chopped stuffed olives
1 teaspoon chopped chives

Thoroughly mix all ingredients. Cover and refrigerate
for at least 1 hour before serving.

POPPY SEED DRESSING

2/3 cup white distilled vinegar
2 teaspoons finely grated onion
1 cup sugar
2 teaspoons dry mustard
2 teaspoons salt
2 cups vegetable oil
3 tablespoons poppy seeds

Combine the vinegar, onion, sugar, mustard and salt in a bowl and stir vigorously with a wire whisk until the sugar, mustard and salt dissolve. Whisking constantly, pour in the oil as a slow, thin stream and continue to beat until the dressing is smooth and thick. Stir in the poppy seeds and taste for seasoning.

Serve the dressing at once with any fruit salad or cover tightly with plastic wrap and store in a cool place or the refrigerator until ready to serve. Tightly covered and refrigerated, the dressing can safely be kept for 6 to 10 days. Makes 2-1/2 cups

CHILE FRENCH DRESSING

1 cup French dressing
2 tablespoons finely chopped chilies
OR 2 tablespoons chile sauce
OR 1/2 teaspoon chili powder

Add chilies to French dressing and mix well. Cover and refrigerate for 1 hour before serving.

CHILE PIMIENTO CHEESE DRESSING

1 cup mayonnaise
1 ounce pimiento cheese, creamed
2 tablespoons chile sauce
1/2 teaspoon Worcestershire sauce

Thoroughly mix all ingredients, cover and refrigerate for 1 hour before serving.

Fruits and Vegetables

Fresh fruits and vegetables for dinner. Nowadays they seem commonplace. But to people born before the time when produce could be grown in California and shipped to supermarkets in Maine, when even canned beans were a novelty, fresh plants for a meal were available only if you had a garden. Corn was the mainstay of frontier gardens. Other crops from subsistence farming included sweet potatoes, cabbages, potatoes, turnips, pumpkins, squash, onions and more. And often as not, gardens were lost to grasshoppers, blackbirds, early frost, or other natural calamities.

Today more and more Americans are going "back to the soil," growing their own produce in backyard gardens. But the plants they grow and the ways they prepare them today are mostly inventions of the twentieth century. Soil and weather patterns have changed. Fruits and vegetables themselves have undergone a transformation over the years of scientific breeding and hybridizing. The modern corn crop now consists almost entirely of a hybrid corn unknown until the 1920's.

Some feel that fruits and vegetables are less flavorful as a result of scientific alterations. But just as some have lost flavor, some have inevitably gained. Most plants are more productive, yielding more food per plant or per acre. Many are more resistant to common diseases and pests.

As fruits and vegetables have changed, so have our ways of preparing them for the table. Today we know about vitamins and do our best not to wash or cook them away. Old West cooks, knowing less about nutrition and more about other problems, were cautious. Soaking fresh-picked produce in spring water and thorough cooking were accepted ways to cook them and to treat possible poisons, pests, and residue from animal manure.

Ways of preserving the harvest influenced the choice of plantings. Root vegetables could be stored where they grew or in the cellar along with thick-skinned squashes, apples and foods that could be dried, like corn and peas. Surplus cucumbers, tomatoes, and beets could be pickled. Today there is a greater emphasis on highly seasonal and perishable delicacies like asparagus and strawberries because they are readily available at the frozen food counter.

After dry cold storage and pickling came the era of home canning. New techniques perfected in 1803 for Napoleon's army were soon applied in commercial canneries. After the Civil War, they became available to the housewife. Canning came into the home with the production of patent jars with lids that could be given an airtight seal. At first they held pickles and other old-fashioned preserves, but in time all kinds of fresh vegetables and fruit were being "put up." Home canning reached its peak with the invention of the kitchen pressure canner.

One of the best known garden fruits was the apple. Only the orange has surpassed it as America's leading cultivated fruit. Seeds brought here from England by the colonists found the climate and soil favorable. In the early 1800's, John Chapman, the legendary Johnny Appleseed, traveled through the Midwest like an apple missionary spreading apple seeds and planting trees. By 1870, more than a thousand native American varieties had been produced by grafting. It was these apples, dried to make them lightweight and long-lasting, that accompanied many pioneers on their long journey to the Old West.

TRAPPER'S FRUIT

Trapper's Fruit, so-called because it was easy for fur trappers of the Old West to carry and prepare, is served in two versions. Version I is a fine dessert; version II is an accompaniment to roasted and broiled meats.

VERSION I

2 pounds of dried apples
2 cups of applesauce
3 tablespoons of honey
1/2 cup of nuts of your choice
2 tablespoons coriander seed
1/2 cup raisins
2 ounces of dark rum
whipped cream with vanilla

Boil the dry apples in applesauce, with honey, nuts, coriander seed and raisins. Cook over medium heat for approximately 15 minutes; then add dark rum. Serve hot in dessert bowls, topped with real whipped cream, flavored with a dash of vanilla. Serves eight.

VERSION II

3 cups coarsely chopped dried apples
1 cup pureed pumpkin
1/2 cup dark brown sugar
1/4 cup roasted sunflower seeds
1/4 cup seedless raisins
1/4 teaspoon coriander seeds
1 teaspoon salt
1 quart water

Combine all ingredients in a heavy 4-quart casserole and mix well. Bring to a boil over high heat, reduce to low, cover tightly and simmer for about 1-1/2 hours, or until the apples are tender. Check occasionally and, if the fruit seems dry, add a little more water. Transfer to a bowl and cool to room temperature before serving.

MOLDED FRUIT SALAD

1 package orange gelatin
1 cup hot water
1 cup whipping cream
1 cup sugar
1 cup crushed pineapple
1 cup of white grapes
2 cups raw ground cranberries

In a large bowl, pour water over orange gelatin. In another bowl, mix sugar and crushed cranberries. After gelatin has cooled, whip until light and frothy. Whip cream until stiff and fold into gelatin. Add cranberry/sugar mixture, pineapple, and grapes (canned pineapple and grapes may be substituted) and chill in a mold.

FRUIT SOUP

1 pound of raisins
1 pound of prunes
1/2 pound currants
1/2 pound red raspberries
6 apples
juice of 1/2 lemon
sugar
cinnamon sticks
1 tablespoon cornstarch

Simmer the raisins, prunes, currants, raspberries, apples and lemon juice together with water for three hours. Add sugar to taste and cinnamon sticks. Then add cornstarch to thicken and cook a few minutes more. Serve either hot or cold. It will keep a long time in the refrigerator. This may be served at the beginning of a meal or as a dessert.

Santa Fe Bob sez:

Vitamin-rich rhubarb was one of the Mormon pioneer mainstays. Settlers traveling west brought rhubarb roots wrapped in dampened cloths, or packed in a can of dirt. The dedication and heroism of these travelers has rarely been equalled. The Mormon culinary heritage has its roots in the British Isles, Scandinavia and Switzerland. Old recipes were adapted to the foods of the Old West. Fruit Soup was a dish that originated in Scandinavia.

RHUBARB CONSERVE

5 pounds rhubarb stalks
grated rind and juice of 2 lemons
grated rind and juice of 2 oranges
8 cups sugar
3 cups cider vinegar
1/2 teaspoon powdered cloves
1 teaspoon cinnamon

Wash rhubarb. Cut into small pieces. Cover with boiling water and let stand 3 minutes. Drain. Add sugar, vinegar, rind and juice of oranges and lemons, and spices. Cook over low heat so as not to scorch. When mixture thickens, pour into hot sterilized canning jars. Process in boiling water bath 10 minutes.

APRICOT RICE PUDDING

3 tablespoons raw rice
1 tablespoon sugar
1 quart milk
1/4 teaspoon salt
3/4 teaspoon cinnamon
1/2 cup soaked dried apricots, diced
2 eggs

Wash rice and combine with all other ingredients except for the eggs.

Separate eggs. Beat egg whites until very stiff. Add beaten egg yolks to egg whites, folding in gently.

Add egg mixture to rice mixture, blending gently. Transfer mixture to a baking pan or casserole and bake in a preheated 250°F. oven for two hours, stirring frequently so mixture does not stick. Makes 6 servings.

CITRUS SALSA

2 large oranges
1 large grapefruit
2 medium-sized tomatoes
2 tablespoons each lime and orange juice
1/4 cup chopped fresh cilantro
1 teaspoon sugar

Cut peel and remove all white membrane from oranges and grapefruit; lift out sections. Coarsely chop fruit. Also peel, core, and chop 2 medium-size tomatoes.

In a bowl, mix oranges, grapefruit, tomatoes, lime and orange juice, cilantro, and sugar.

Season to taste with salt. If made ahead, cover and refrigerate until next day. This tangy mixture goes well with grilled fish or poultry. Makes 3 cups.

FRUIT TOSTADAS

These Tostada baskets are always a big hit and a creative way to serve fresh summer fruits.

2 quarts vegetable oil
one dozen 10-inch flour tortillas
12 cups fresh summer fruits—use a variety of colors,
shapes, and sizes such as melon balls, strawberries,
blueberries, and pineapple wedges or banana rounds
1/4 cup cactus honey or strong-flavored blossom honey
1/4 cup freshly squeezed lime juice

Heat the oil to 375°F. in an electric deep-fat fryer or in a deep heavy pot, using a thermometer to maintain the correct temperature.

Fry the tortillas, using the compuesta ("little basket") technique. The simplest way is to use a tostada frying basket. To fry, place the tortilla in the basket on top of the hot oil. The edges of the tortilla will flute up around the edges of the basket. Drain the fried tostada shells on absorbent paper towels.

Prepare the fruit and place all together in a large bowl. Combine the honey and lime juice. Pour over the fruit and carefully stir to coat the fruit; do not bruise it. Chill until just ready to serve. You can let it marinate up to 2 hours, but not more than that as the fruits will start to droop.

Warm the tostada baskets in a 250°F. oven for 10 to 15 minutes, or until warm and crisp. To serve, place the marinated fruits in the tostada baskets. Try to spoon the fruits in carefully, and artistically arrange the top of each basket. Distribute the juice evenly. Serve immediately. Serves 12.

PEAR RELISH

Here's a relish that tastes like bread and butter pickles and ages well. It is much better 3 months after you put it up than it was the first week. Use Kieffer or old field pears, and choose pears that are full-sized but still hard.

12 good-sized hard pears
4 cups onions
4 cups green bell pepper
1/2 cup jalapeño peppers
4 cups sweet red bell peppers
4 cups white sugar
6 tablespoons powdered mustard
2 tablespoons powdered turmeric
5 tablespoons salt
2 quarts apple cider vinegar
cayenne pepper to taste

Peel pears and chop finely in a food processor or put through a grinder by hand. Chop onions very fine. Peel and seed the peppers and cut fine. Mix pears, onions, and peppers in a colander. Drain, but do not squeeze. Place in a deep enameled kettle. Add remaining ingredients except cayenne.

Place over low heat and bring to a slow boil, stirring occasionally. Cook for 30 minutes, stirring from time to time. Remove from heat and add cayenne pepper to taste. Seal in hot sterile pints. Process in boiling water bath 15 minutes. Makes 12 pints.

PICKLED PEACHES

Since it's more than likely you'll be buying your peaches, you may as well get exactly what you want. Peaches for the market are graded by size—so many to the box. The larger the peach, the more they charge for the box. But you really don't need the biggest peaches. In fact, be sure the peaches you pick will fit through the top of a Mason jar. So you can go for a smaller, less expensive peach and get a box of uniform-sized peaches that will fit the jars and won't cost nearly as much as the big ones sold in the grocery store. Size 70 is the ideal size to buy. This means there are 70 peaches to the 30-pound box. It is strictly a matter of personal preference, but white-meat peaches for pickling, make a juice that is a wonderful clear ruby color. Ask for clingstone peaches. If you decide to pickle an entire 30-pound box of peaches, multiply this recipe times 6 and expect 18 quarts.

5 pounds clingstone peaches
1 teaspoon whole cloves plus 1 clove per peach
1/2 ounce stick cinnamon plus 1 stick per jar
1 teaspoon whole allspice
1-1/2 cups apple cider vinegar (50 grain)
1/2 cup water
4 cups sugar

Slip skins from peaches. Insert a clove in each peach. Make a cloth bag to hold remaining spices and tie with a clean cotton string. Combine vinegar, water, and sugar. Bring to a boil. Add spice bag. Cook peaches in this juice, a few at a time until tender to the touch of a fork (no more than 5 minutes usually). As soon as peaches are cooked, place them in hot sterilized jars. Once you've cooked all the peaches, reduce juice by half. Pour over peaches. Place one stick of cinnamon in each jar. Wipe rim with clean cloth. Seal. Process in boiling water bath 15 minutes. Makes 3 quarts.

MINTED MEXICAN FRUITS
IN MELON BASKET

It takes a little time to create an attractive basket and it's just a bit labor-intensive, but this traditional dish is perfect for big parties. For a festive occasion a big, deep green watermelon is perfect. Twin honeydew baskets cut in sharp zigzags are also attractive if you need smaller containers. The melons and other fruits will have the fullest flavor if marinated at least 2 hours at room temperature and then chilled, but they should not be held more than 4 hours total.

1 large watermelon, 16 to 18 inches long
1 cup water
1-1/2 cups strong-flavored blossom honey
juice of 2 fresh limes
1 cup fresh mint leaves, well rinsed and mashed
1 medium honeydew melon
1 medium cantaloupe
1 large, ripe pineapple
2 long cucumbers
3 papayas
grape or citrus leaves for garnish, optional

Use a long chef's knife to cut into the longest side of the watermelon about two-thirds of the way up the melon. and one-third of the way into it. Make a similar cut from the other side. Then slice down one-third of the way to meet the lengthwise cuts, creating a 2-1/2-inch-wide handle—being very, very careful not to cut too deep or too far down as ripe watermelon. If you use too much pressure you can cause the melon to crack. Using a grease marking pencil or a dull pointed knife to score the pattern you wish to follow may make the cutting a little easier. Once you are pleased with your cutting, remove the two pieces of watermelon carefully, rind and all. Even out any ragged cutting areas and cut out the watermelon flesh under the handle. Make even scallops all the way around the two lengthwise top sides. Leave the handle with straight sides. Chill overnight. Reserve the watermelon fruit for making melon balls.

To prepare the honey-mint sauce heat the water in a small saucepan. When it is simmering, add the honey. As soon as the honey starts to melt, remove from the heat. Add the lime juice and the mashed whole mint leaves, reserving about 6 mint sprigs for garnish. Set aside at room temperature.

About 5 hours or less before the party, make the melon balls and prepare the other fruits. Use the large side of the melon bailer to scoop out the watermelon from the basket. Put the basket back into the refrigerator. Use the smaller side to make honeydew and cantaloupe balls. Cut the pineapple in half, peel, and slice into 1-inch-thick slices being sure to remove the woody core. Cut into 1-inch wedges.

Peel the cucumbers, then cut them horizontally into thirds. Cut each third in half, then into long thin sticks—similar to carrot sticks.

Peel the papayas, cut in half, and remove the seeds, then cut all the way across each half, creating half-moons. These cutting instructions insure that each fruit has its own shape, making an interesting display when the basket is served.

Place all the fruit in a very large bowl deep enough to allow stirring. Carefully drizzle the honey-mint sauce over the fruit, being sure to cover as much fruit as possible. Allow to set. Then occasionally stir, taking great care not to break up the pieces of fruit. Cover and set out of the way. Once the fruit has set out for 2 hours, chill it until ready to serve. To serve, carefully spoon the fruits into the watermelon basket. Save back an equal assortment of each fruit for topping it off. Then place on a large silver platter or any other large tray. Place the reserved mint sprigs randomly across the top. Garnish the tray with grape leaves, if available, or any broad pretty leaf such as a poplar, orange, or other citrus—even Romaine lettuce. For an added touch, tie a brightly-colored bow around the melon handle. Makes 14 to 16 servings.

CRANBERRY SALSA

2 large oranges
2 cups fresh cranberries
4 teaspoons grated orange peel
1/4 cup minced onion
1/4 cup vegetable oil
1 tablespoon each minced fresh cilantro and ginger
1 small hot chile, stemmed, seeded and minced

Cut, peel and remove all white membrane from oranges; lift out sections. Coarsely chop orange sections. Using a knife or a food processor, coarsely chop cranberries.

In a bowl, combine all ingredients and mix thoroughly. Season to taste with salt. If made ahead, cover and refrigerate for up to 2 days. Makes about 3 cups. Serve with poultry, lamb or pork.

CANTALOUPE MARMALADE

1 medium-size ripe cantaloupe
1 large lemon
1 large navel orange
1 cup crushed or minced pineapple, preferably fresh
granulated sugar

Peel the cantaloupe, remove the seeds, and coarsely process fruit in a food processor or blender, or chop rather fine.

Quarter the lemon and orange. Slice paper thin using great care and a very sharp knife. Hand slicing works better here than using a machine.

Measure the quantity of fruit and add 3/4 cup sugar for each cup of fruit. Place in a large crock or porcelain-lined heavy pot. Allow to marinate overnight.

Place the fruit in a heavy preserving kettle. Cook, stirring frequently, for 45 minutes, or until thick and bubbly. Meanwhile, sterilize the jars and serving container you wish to use by placing them in a large pot with 1 inch of water. Boil, remove from heat, and allow to almost cool.

Skim the marmalade with a metal spoon. Place in sterilized jars and seal with paraffin. It is not necessary to add the paraffin if you wish to serve within a day or two.

To serve, place the cooled marmalade in a glass bowl, or even a footed compote. It makes a great brunch addition.

TROPICAL FRUIT-STUFFED PINEAPPLE

1 very large pineapple
1 mango, peeled and cut into half circles
1 papaya, watermelon or pink type, cut into squares
1 pint whole ripe strawberries(if not available, substitute red seedless grapes)
12 fresh orange or lemon leaves, optional

To prepare the pineapple, use a large, sharp cutting knife or an electric knife. Hold the pineapple upright by the top and slice all the way through the leaves down into the flesh, completely cutting all the way through into two halves. Then cut each half into three equal parts.

Next, starting at the base of each sixth, cut the flesh evenly away from the rind, cutting close enough to the rind to get a nice deep, fleshy portion, but without too many eyes. Cut each in two equal lengthwise parts, then cut into 3/4-inch-wide crosswise slices.

On a large platter place alternating slices of pineapple, one to the left, the next to the right, in a "herring bone" pattern. The rest of the tropical fruits and strawberries should be artfully arranged over the pineapple. Garnish with leaves if available.

OLD-FASHIONED
BAKED APPLE BUTTER

8 cups apples
1 cup cider
2-1/2 cups sugar
1 teaspoon ground cinnamon
1 teaspoon ground allspice
1 teaspoon ground cloves

Peel, core, and chop apples. In a large saucepan or kettle bring chopped apples and cider to a rapid boil. Reduce heat and simmer until apples are soft and pulpy, about 20 minutes. Strain pulp through a sieve. Blend sugar into hot pulp. Mix in spices. Pour into a casserole dish or baking pan. Cover loosely with foil. Bake in 400° F. oven for 1 hour. Stir frequently until apple butter is thick enough for spreading. Pour into sterilized jars and seal. Process in boiling water bath for 15 minutes.

SAVORY BAKED SQUASH RINGS

2 medium acorn squashes
1/3 cup pineapple juice
1/2 stick butter or margarine
2 teaspoons grated lemon rind
1/2 cup brown sugar
dash salt
1/4 cup corn syrup

Slice off tops of squashes and scoop out seeds and pulp. Cut squash into 1/4-inch rings. Arrange rings in a baking dish. Pour pineapple juice over rings. Cover dish and bake in moderate (350° F.) oven 30 minutes. Remove from oven. Make a mixture of butter. lemon rind, brown sugar, salt and corn syrup and pour over rings. Bake 15 minutes more.

PARCHED CORN CASSEROLE

Parched corn is green corn that has been shaved from the ears and sun-dried. It was an item that used to be carried in grocery stores in 5-pound cloth bags. To parch your own corn, take freshly shucked and cleaned corn and dip ears in lightly salted boiling water. Shave off the kernels, being careful not to get the cob. Sprinkle the kernels on a cheesecloth frame and dry in the sun or use a home dehydrator. When perfectly flaky, use a rolling pin to press flat and store for future use. OR, you can substitute canned cream-style corn.

1-1/2 cups parched corn
1/4 pound cubed salt pork
2 large potatoes
2 slices dry bread
1 cup of milk
salt and pepper
1 small sliced onion
1 quart water

Put on water to boil. Add the onions and salt pork. Sift in the parched corn, stirring all the while, then simmer under a cover. Boil the potatoes in a separate pan. Watch the potatoes and put them in cold water to cool when they are on the hard side of being done. Cut into 1/2-inch cubes, and add to the corn chowder. Add the milk. Salt and pepper to taste. Simmer.

If timed correctly, the corn will be done, and the potatoes, while done, will be firm rather than cooked into a mush. Heavily butter the bread and toast on a hot griddle. The toasting will allow the bread to be cut, hot, into cubes. Serve in a buttered casserole dish and garnish with the toast cubes.

BAKED STUFFED PUMPKIN

Many traditional Southwest Indian recipes called for some kind of squash which comes in a variety of forms. Most Indian homes usually had a storage area where chunks of dried squash were kept. Here is a delicious recipe that calls for one of the most recognizable kinds of squash-the pumpkin.

1 large pumpkin
3 tablespoons margarine or butter
salt to taste
2 cups corn, fresh or canned
2 cups chopped green beans
1 pound ground sirloin
2 onions
2 peeled and cubed peaches
1 cup cooked chicken meat
1 cup hulled, toasted sunflower seeds
1 cup chopped green bell pepper

Cut a fairly wide lid from the top of a large pumpkin and scrape out all the seeds and strings. Butter, salt and pepper the inside and place without the lid in an oven preheated to 350°F. Bake for 40 minutes and be sure to use a long ladle to empty the liquid that will accumulate on the inside of the pumpkin, otherwise it may collapse.

Brown the ground sirloin and onion in a skillet. Now add the sirloin and onions and all other ingredients and bake for about another hour adding just enough water to keep moist. Salt and pepper to taste. Serve the entire pumpkin and be sure to spoon out the cooked walls of the pumpkin when serving.

GREEN CHILE AND POTATOES

1 tablespoon vegetable oil
1 medium, chopped onion
1 chopped garlic clove
4 green chilies, chopped,
OR 1/4 cup chopped frozen chilies
2 cups diced potatoes
salt to taste
boiling water

Prepare chilies. Cook potatoes until tender, but not mushy. Lightly sauté onion and garlic, add chopped chilies and diced potatoes. If cooked potatoes are used, add water to cover and boil 10 minutes. Serves 4.

GREEN CHILE AND SQUASH

7 to 12 green chilies,
OR 1/2 cup frozen chilies
2 cups cubed summer squash
1 small onion
salt to taste
1 cup fresh or frozen corn (optional)
1 tablespoon fat

Clean and prepare chilies. Remove stems and seeds. Lightly saute chopped onion, add squash and corn. Cook slowly in little or no water until tender. Add chopped chilies, salt, and serve. Makes 6 to 8 servings.

HERDSMAN'S POTATOES

3 tablespoons bacon fat or vegetable oil
9 medium-sized boiling potatoes (about 3 pounds)
salt
freshly ground black pepper
4 eggs
2 tablespoons finely cut fresh chives
1 tablespoon finely chopped fresh parsley
1/4 teaspoon crumbled dried thyme

Evenly heat 2 tablespoons of bacon fat or vegetable oil in a 10-inch heavy frying pan. Arrange about one third of the potato slices in a flat layer in the skillet and season them lightly with salt and pepper. Repeat two more times, then dribble or dot the remaining tablespoon of bacon fat or vegetable oil over the top. Cover tightly and bake in the middle of the oven preheated to 375°F. for about 1 hour, or until the potatoes are tender.

Beat the eggs lightly with a wire whisk or a fork, add the chives, parsley and thyme, and mix well. Then pour the egg mixture over the potatoes, cover again and continue baking for 5 minutes, or until the eggs are just firm to the touch. Do not over cook.

To unmold and serve the potatoes, loosen the edges by running a knife or spatula around the sides of the frying pan and as far beneath the potatoes as possible without breaking them apart. Place an inverted plate on top of the skillet and, grasping plate and skillet together firmly, turn them over. The potatoes should slide out easily. Serve at once.

OKRA AND TOMATOES

1 pound fresh or frozen (defrosted) okra
4 lean slices bacon, cut crosswise in half
1 medium-sized chopped onion
1-1/2 teaspoons salt
3 medium-sized firm, ripe tomatoes
1 teaspoon fresh hot red chilies, finely chopped

Wash the fresh okra under cold running water, and with a small sharp knife scrape the skin lightly to remove any surface fuzz. Frozen okra needs only to be thoroughly defrosted and drained. Pat the okra completely dry with paper towels, cut off the stems and slice crosswise into 1/2 inch-thick rounds. Peel and coarsely chop tomatoes.

In a heavy 10-inch skillet, fry the bacon over moderate heat, turning the pieces frequently with tongs until they are crisp and brown and have rendered all their fat. Transfer the bacon to paper towels to drain.

Add the okra, onion and salt to the fat remaining in the skillet and, stirring constantly, cook over moderate heat for 10 minutes. Watch carefully and regulate the heat so that the vegetables do not burn. Add the tomatoes and chili and cook over high heat for 2 minutes, still stirring constantly. Reduce the heat to low and, stirring the mixture occasionally, simmer uncovered for about 15 minutes, or until the okra and tomatoes are soft. Season to taste.

To serve, transfer the entire contents of the skillet to a heated bowl and arrange the bacon on top. Serves 4.

Santa Fe Bob sez:

Although a staple of diet, the bean was not highly prized by those who ate their meals on the trail. Of course, some cooks were inspired with beans, but the term "sowbelly and bean outfit" was derogatory. Cowboys agreed that the farther north they traveled the better the grub, and the fewer the beans. The cheap, rough-cooking blackeye, pinto, and dark beans were favored by the owners, if not the cooks and cowboys, of outfits down toward the Rio Grande. Firehole Beans was a cowboy name for dark beans prepared in the "Boston-baked" manner. "Firehole" in this case was not related to the method of cooking, but was a mispronunciation of the Spanish word for beans or frijoles.

Halved, baked potatoes were favorites with settlers in the early days even though ovens were in short supply in the Old West. Some owned portable army stoves, which they set up on bases of home-baked clay, and the trading posts stocked the little, one-lidded Prospector's Friend.

FIRE HOLE BEANS

1 quart black beans
1/2 pound salt pork
3 quarts water
2/3 cup blackstrap molasses
1 rounded tablespoon salt
1 teaspoon dry mustard
1 can tomatoes

Soak beans overnight. Pour off the water and transfer to a heavy iron pot or dutch oven equipped with a tight-fitting lid. Add salt and cold water. Bring slowly to a boil and keep boiling for 3 hours, being sure to add water if the level gets to low. Slice the salt pork into one inch cubes. Add pork ,molasses, mustard and tomatoes. Cover and bake. If cooking on a campfire, a shovelful of coals should be kept on the lid. Bake all day or all night making sure there is a small amount of liquid on the top.

GOLDEN BAKED POTATOES

potatoes
butter, margarine or bacon fat
paprika

Cut each potato in half lengthwise. Score the faces about 1/4 inch deep using the point of a knife. Press on a dry paper towel until all possible moisture is removed. Spread with butter, margarine or bacon fat. Sprinkle lightly with paprika.
Rub with the thumb until the oily coating turns orange from paprika and the cross-scoring comes into view. Bake,scored side up, in hot oven until done. The tops will puff, crust over, and assume a beautiful golden brown.

HOPPING JOHN

Blackeye beans, or cowpeas, were named Hopping John because they grew so fast they seemed to hop right out of the ground. Now the term is applied to a stewed mixture of beans, peppers, and rice. The following is a standard recipe used by cowboy camp cooks.

1 quart blackeye beans
3/4 quart rice
2 ham hocks or one pound of chopped bacon
1 dried hot pepper
1 tablespoon salt
water

Pour the blackeye beans (cowpeas) into salted, boiling water and immediately set aside to cool. Boil the ham hocks for 2 hours. Drain the beans and add them to the ham hocks. Simmer for about 1 hour, or until the beans are tender.

Add the rice and crushed red pepper. Be sure there is sufficient liquid because rice requires three to four times its bulk. If using ham hocks, when the rice is done, take out the hocks and allow to cool slightly. Remove the lean meat and serve with the Hopping John.

You can substitute a large can of tomatoes and 1/2 cup or more of butter or margarine for ham or bacon to make an excellent variation of this recipe.

CORN WITH PINTO BEANS

1 cup dry pinto beans
2 cups frozen corn kernels
1/2 pound salt pork, diced
1 medium-sized onion, chopped
1 tablespoon lard or vegetable oil

In a large heavy saucepan, place pinto beans, corn, and salt pork in water to cover and bring to a boil. Simmer for 2 hours or until tender.

Sauté onion in lard or oil. Add to beans and corn mixture and serve. Makes 6 servings.

SUCCOTASH

3 cups canned pinto beans, drained
1-1/2 cups fresh or frozen corn kernels
1-1/2 cups fresh string beans, chopped
1-1/2 cups water
4 tablespoons butter, margarine or shortening
1 teaspoon sugar
1 teaspoon salt
pepper to taste
2 tablespoons shelled sunflower seeds, crushed

Place all the ingredients, except for the sunflower seeds, in water in a large heavy saucepan with 2 tablespoons butter. Simmer for 15 minutes or until vegetables are tender.

Add sunflower seeds and remaining butter. Continue to simmer until mixture thickens. Makes 6 servings.

TEQUILA LIME SWEET POTATOES

3/4 cup butter or margarine
2 pounds sweet potatoes
2 tablespoons brown sugar
2 tablespoons tequila
1 tablespoon lime juice
salt and pepper
lime wedges

Melt butter in a 14-inch frying pan and set aside. Peel sweet potatoes and shred using a food processor or coarse side of a hand grater. Mix with butter in pan and sprinkle in sugar. Cook over medium heat about 15 minutes until potatoes begin to caramelize and begin to appear slightly translucent. Turn occasionally with a spatula.

Add tequila and lime juice. Cook for 3 more minutes, stirring occasionally. Season with salt and pepper. Serve in a bowl garnished with lime. Makes 6 to 8 servings.

CHILI SQUASH

3 medium-sized squash, diced
2 onions, chopped
1 clove garlic, minced
4 tablespoons butter or vegetable oil
1 cup tomato puree
1 small can tomato paste
1 sweet red pepper
1 small can green chilies, sliced
2 teaspoons ground red chili

In a large heavy skillet, sauté squash, onions, and garlic over low heat in butter or oil until squash is lightly browned.

Add remaining ingredients and simmer, covered, for 30 minutes. Makes 6 servings.

BAKED PUMPKIN

1 medium-sized pumpkin, peeled and cubed
1 cup brown sugar
1 teaspoon melted butter
cinnamon

Place pumpkin in a baking pan and sprinkle with sugar and butter. Cover pan with foil and bake in a preheated 350°F. oven for 30 minutes or until tender.
Serve topped with cinnamon. Makes 4 servings.

ZUCCHINI CASSEROLE

1-3 to 4 pound zucchini, washed and sliced thin
salt
1/4 cup butter or olive oil
2 cloves pressed garlic
2 chopped onions
oregano
cilantro
coarsely ground pepper
4 ripe, thin-sliced tomatoes
2 cups grated Swiss cheese

Slice zucchini very thin, salt generously, and place in a colander. Let stand for about 30 minutes to drain water. Rinse salt off, then pat zucchini dry.
Cover the bottom of a 10" x 13" Pyrex utility pan with half of sliced zucchini. Sauté the garlic and onion in butter or olive oil. Sprinkle zucchini with moderate amounts of oregano, cilantro, and pepper. Place thin tomato slices over zucchini. Then add half of the sautéed onion, garlic, and olive oil (or butter). Repeat layers. Top with cheese. Bake uncovered at 350° F. for 30-45 minutes, until the top is glazed and golden brown. Serves 6.

SPICED RED CABBAGE

6 cups shredded red cabbage
1 teaspoon salt
3 tablespoons melted butter
1/4 cup sugar
1 tart chopped apple
1/4 cup water
6 whole cloves
3 tablespoons vinegar

Combine all ingredients, except the vinegar. Pour into a buttered casserole dish. Bake in 325° F. oven 30-40 minutes, or until cabbage is tender. Sprinkle vinegar over cabbage immediately upon removing dish from oven. Makes 6 servings.

ROASTED ONIONS

3/4 cup water
1/2 cup balsamic or red wine vinegar
2 teaspoons firmly packed brown sugar
1/8 teaspoon pepper
4 medium-size onions
salt

Blend the water, vinegar, sugar, and pepper. Pour into a 9 x 13-inch baking pan. Cut onions in half lengthwise through skins; place, cut side down, in vinegar mixture.

Bake, uncovered, in lower third of a 400°F. oven until onions give readily when gently squeezed and cut sides are glazed (1 to 1-1/4 hours). Arrange, cut side up, on a platter. Season to taste with salt. Goes well with roast beef, turkey, pork chops, or sausages. Makes 8 servings.

EGGPLANT SOUFFLÉ

1 eggplant
2 tablespoons butter or margarine
2 tablespoons flour
1 cup warm milk
3/4 cup bread crumbs
2 teaspoons grated onion
1 tablespoon catsup
1 teaspoon salt
1 cup grated Cheddar cheese
2 eggs, separated

Peel and cut eggplant into chunks. Place in saucepan with just enough water to cover and cook until soft. Drain and mash eggplant. Set aside. Make a light thickening with butter and flour by melting butter in small pan, then adding flour and stirring until golden. Add milk, cook and stir until you have a nice white sauce.

Now add mashed eggplant, bread, onion, catsup, salt, cheese, and egg yolks. Beat whites until they hold firm peaks, then fold into first mixture. Turn into a well-greased baking dish. Put dish into a pan of water and bake at 375°F. for 45 minutes—or until the souffle has set (it shouldn't jiggle when you tap the side).

In making this or any other souffle choose a 1-1/2 quart round casserole dish and make a sort of lip around it with a long piece of aluminum foil, folded over lengthwise and fitted around the edge of the dish to extend the sides up at least 2 inches. This will guide the soufflé in the right direction and makes any soufflé picture-perfect. Remove foil to serve. Makes 6 to 8 servings.

ZUCCHINI WITH CORN AND PEPPERS

3 tablespoons butter or margarine
2-1/2 pounds zucchini, cut into 1/4-inch slice
1-1/2 cups fresh corn kernels, or 1 package (10 oz.)
frozen whole-kernel corn, thawed
1 red bell pepper, seeded and chopped
1 medium-size onion, chopped
2 cloves garlic, minced or pressed
salt and pepper

Melt butter in a wide frying pan over high heat; add zucchini, corn, bell pepper, onion, and garlic.

Cook, stirring often, until vegetables are tender but crisp to bite (about 5 minutes). Season to taste with salt and pepper. Makes 8 to 10 servings.

PUMPKIN BUTTER

2 16-ounce cans pumpkin
1-1/2 cups brown sugar
1 teaspoon grated lemon peel
1/4 teaspoon cinnamon
1 teaspoon grated orange peel
1/4 teaspoon ginger
1/2 cup orange juice
1/4 teaspoon ground cloves
1/2 cup lemon juice
1/4 teaspoon salt

Combine all ingredients in a heavy saucepan. Cook over low fire until desired thickness is reached. Stir constantly to prevent scorching. Let cool. Pour into sterilized jars and refrigerate. Great with hot breads and biscuits.

BEET PICKLES

Dark-red beet pickles really gave the typical Sunday dinner plate heaped with chicken pie, gravy, baked beans, and salt pork an interesting look as well as a refreshing taste.

"Beet pickles" refers to a home canning product that was prized for its bright color as well as its sweet and sour flavor. "Pickled beets" were made more simply by cooking and slicing the beets, then soaking them overnight in vinegar water to serve the next day.

Small beets, four or five to the pound, make the best pickles. Buy them with stems and green tops (three pounds in all) to make sure they are fresh and not from cold storage.

> 2 pounds of beets, trimmed of leaves
> 1 cup of granulated sugar
> 1 cup of cider vinegar
> 1/2 teaspoon salt
> pinch of pepper
> 6 whole cloves

Trim beets and scrub them clean. Boil in kettle or saucepan in enough water to cover (2 to 3 cups) until beets are tender. This may take 20 to 40 minutes. Set beets aside to cool; pour away all but 1 cup of the liquid. Add to it sugar and vinegar; boil briskly until thickening starts, about 5 minutes.

Meanwhile skin beets with a table knife and cut crosswise in slices 1/8-inch thick. Add slices, salt, and pepper to syrup and heat again, just to boiling. Sterilize canning jars. Using funnel and slotted spoon, transfer slices into jars. Add 2 cloves to each jar, ladle in hot liquid to fill jars, and seal. When they are cool, label and date jars and remove them to cool, dark shelf for at least two weeks. Makes 3 pints.

GREEN TOMATO AND CHEESE PIE

9-inch prebaked pie shell
1 cup onions, chopped
1 cup green pepper, chopped
1 clove garlic, minced
3 tablespoons vegetable oil
5 to 6 medium green tomatoes
2 tablespoons flour
2 tablespoons salt
1/8 teaspoon pepper
1 cup Cheddar cheese, shredded
parsley flakes

Sauté onions, green pepper and garlic in vegetable oil in a large skillet. Cut tomatoes into chunks and add to onions, pepper and garlic.

Cook over hot fire 12-15 minutes, stirring frequently. Stir in flour, salt and pepper until blended. Pour mixture into pie shell. Spread grated cheese evenly over tomatoes. Sprinkle with parsley flakes. Bake in hot (400° F.) oven about 15 minutes or until top is nicely browned. Makes 6 to 8 servings.

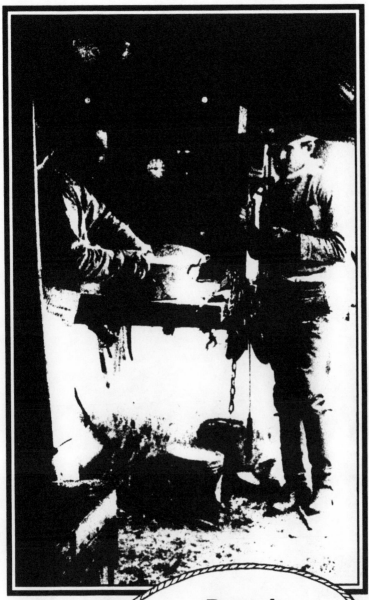

Breads

Making bread is a real kitchen adventure. Yeast is a living thing that grows at different rates. The same recipe often yields different results. There are other variables. The moisture content in flour varies—even in flour from the same sack from one day to the next. The weather varies. Bread making in the Old West was a highly-valued skill and very much an art.

The untreated flours and meals used in the Old West often got weevils. It's true, in the old days when flour was bought in 100 pound sacks, weevils were a constant problem. But there was a simple, old-fashioned way to get rid of them-the sifter.

Weevils aren't cockroaches. They won't hurt you. This sounds horrible, but remember that pesticides are a fairly new invention and that our pioneer ancestors managed to survive in spite of these small pests.

For most of us today, bread making is a luxury. Few of us are home long enough to go through the process that—although it takes only moments of active involvement from time to time—requires hours of attention (especially for sourdough breads).

Tortillas and sopaipillas are the "staffs of life" most frequently accompanying Southwestern-style meals. Tortillas are the best-known bread. Wheat-flour tortillas are generally served as a bread more often than the corn varieties. Corn tortillas are the basis for many main dishes such as enchiladas, tacos and flautas. They are served hot with butter and folded to sop up extra sauce.

Sopaipillas have become very popular outside of Albuquerque where they originated. The hollow inside, surrounded by a thin layer of golden, crispy deep-fried bread, makes them ideal for spreading with honey and jams. The combination of fried bread with sweet honey is a perfect balance for the hot flavors generated by chilies. The flavors are very complementary even if the chilies are not hot. Fats and sugars were traditionally used to calm down the fiery dishes of the Southwest. Fried foods, butter, milk, honey and jams are some of the best recommended accompaniments to spicy meals.

Other more unusual but great-tasting breads are the Navajo fry bread and Moyettes. Fry bread is similar to sopaipillas, only it is not hollow. It is made in large rounds, perfect for serving as a bread or as a holder for fillings such as taco preparations. Moyettes are small cinnamon topped loaves, baked in hornos, the traditional beehive-shaped outdoor ovens to be found in every New Mexico native's backyard.

The woodstove baking techniques that had to be mastered by pioneer cooks resulted in some very tempting recipes that have been handed down from those early days. Gingerbread and Swedish crackers were among the specialties baked by cooks who'd tell you today that bread baked in a real woodburning stove cannot be improved upon by modern conveniences.

SOURDOUGH STARTER

Making sourdough starter is very easy. You can do it in about a minute!

> 2 cups of unbleached flour
> 2-1/2 cups of lukewarm water

Put flour into a crock, jar, or Tupperware bowl that is at least warm to room temperature. Never use a metal container. The bowl should be scalded before using to inhibit the growth of unwanted bacteria. Add 2-1/2 cups lukewarm water, and set the whole batch in a warm but not hot place. That's it.

It is a good idea to have a loose-fitting lid for the pot, to keep the dust out of the working starter. The pot should never be tightly closed because the mixture has to attract yeast spores from the surrounding air.

In about four or five days, the pot will be bubbling slowly and a wonderful aroma will fill your kitchen.

Or you can help it along. Replace the lukewarm water with warm water from boiled potatoes. Or sprinkle a package of active dry yeast over the flour before you mix in the warm water. This will get a starter going in only a few hours.

To keep a starter going all the time, you must remember to replenish what you use with fresh flour and water. Sourdough starter can be kept for several weeks in the refrigerator, and frozen for even longer. You must always bring it back to room temperature until it starts working again before it can be used. In cold weather, starters can lose some potency, but a tablespoon of cider vinegar will revive it nicely.

SECRETS OF GREAT SOURDOUGH

If you want real old-time sourdough, do not use yeast. The less yeast used, the richer and headier the sourdough, but the longer it takes and the trickier the recipes are. For example, real sourdough bread does not have any yeast in either the starter or the bread dough mix. Neither does sourdough French bread, but that's almost too difficult to handle in the average home kitchen, so recipes have been developed using yeast. Some French bread recipes take as long as 24 hours to complete. Sourdough cooking requires a little more heat or a little more time than ordinary baking.

STARTER TIPS

1. Always use unbleached flour and put only flour and water back in the starter pot, don't add any sugar, salt, eggs, soda, or cooking oil. If your starter turns orange, throw it away! Use lukewarm water, never hot or cold water.

2. Remember sourdough bread and pastries can be kept indefinitely in your freezer; they even improve with age!

3. Avoid mixing the batter too much. Over-mixing releases gases which are needed for the raising process from the dough.

4. Baking soda turns sourdough yellow, you may want to use baking powder instead.

5. Wheat flour in starter doesn't rise as much but it works a little faster than white flour.

6. The batter should always be at room temperature when you use it.

7. When making starter, first warm the pot with hot water.

MILK STARTER

Although a starter is simply flour and water, there are many ways to make it. Most sourdough cooks develop their own methods. Here's a common variation.

Let a cup of milk stand for a day or so in an uncovered container at room temperature. Then add a cup of flour, mix, and let stand for another couple of days or until it starts fermenting. It's now ready to use.

Santa Fe Bob sez:

The chuckwagon cook would have the breakfast dishes washed and things packed and ready for a move of ten to fifteen miles by 5:00 a.m. Hopefully the next roundup spot was on a well-defined trail, but many times the trail was full of unexpected events: breakdowns, streams to ford, runaways, or quicksand. The cook had to deal with all of this often with the pan of dough for the next meal under his watchful eye!

Camp cooks kept their sourdough starter in sturdy kegs and protected it carefully because once developed it might never be produced again. Fluctuations in temperature (the sun beating down during the day, and freezing at night) were the greatest threat. In the heat, especially in a rocking wagon, the starter would boil over and work itself stale. The cold would paralyze it. On cold nights the cook would wrap his starter in his own blanket or build a special fire to keep it warm. Cooks kept their favorite starters going for years, but it wasn't easy.

HONEY-WHEAT GERM SOURDOUGH

1 cup sourdough starter
1/4 cup honey
2 cups warm water
7 cups all-purpose flour
2 cups warm milk
1/4 cup wheat germ
1 tablespoon butter
2 tablespoons sugar
1 package dry yeast
2 teaspoons salt
2 teaspoons baking soda

Mix starter and 2-1/2 cups of the flour and all the water the night before. Next morning mix butter with warm milk, and stir in yeast until dissolved. Add honey, and when thoroughly mixed, add 2 more cups flour, and stir in the wheat germ.

Sprinkle sugar, salt, and baking soda over the mixture. Gently press into dough and mix lightly. Allow to stand from 30 to 50 minutes until mixture is bubbly. Add flour until dough cannot be stirred, then place on floured board and knead 100 times or until silky mixture is developed. Form into four 1-pound loaves, place in well-greased loaf pans, size 9 x 2 3/4, and let rise until double—about 2 or 3 hours in a warm room.

Bake at 400°F. for 20 minutes. Reduce oven temperature to 325°F. and bake 20 minutes longer or until thoroughly baked. Remove from pans and place on a rack to cool. A little butter on top of the loaves will prevent them from becoming too crusty.

SOURDOUGH RAISIN BREAD

Simply add raisins (do it the night before) to the sour-dough starter you plan to use in your regular sourdough bread recipe. Be sure to use a bigger bowl than usual to hold the working starter, because the raisins make it rise more.

Then make your bread using the starter with the raisins. You can also make raisin bread rolls and raisin hotcakes the same way, by first filling the starter you're using with raisins and leaving overnight.

SPOON BREAD

1 cup yellow or white corn meal
1 teaspoon baking powder
1/2 teaspoon salt
1 heaping tablespoon butter or margarine
1-1/2 cups canned milk
yolks of 3 eggs, beaten

Mix the corn meal, butter, and a little bit of boiling water to dissolve and make smooth. Let cool. Add egg yolks, well beaten, then the baking powder. The milk should be scalded slightly, but do not boil. Then add the stiffly beaten egg whites. The batter will be thin.

Pour into a well-greased baking dish 2 inches deep. Bake 30 minutes at 425°F. The spoon bread will be soft inside, brown outside. Dip out in large tablespoonful and serve on a heated platter.

SOURDOUGH PUMPERNICKEL

Settlers of European background brought this recipe to the Old West and it's still a specialty in areas where the descendants of these settlers still live. It is difficult to make, but well worth the effort. You shouldn't try this one until you have practiced on other sourdough breads.

You'll find this homemade pumpernickel is totally unlike anything you can buy at the supermarket. It's great for parties, for snacks and lunches. It goes best with cheeses, sausages, salami, and other goodies, including cold dark beer in frosted mugs.

1-1/2 cups sourdough starter
2 cups unsifted rye flour
2 tablespoons chopped caraway seeds
1/2 cup boiling hot black coffee

Pour boiling coffee over chopped caraway seeds. Let mixture cool. Thoroughly mix flour and starter and add coffee and caraway. Let stand for 4 to 8 hours in a warm place, preferably overnight.

1/2 cup molasses
3 tablespoons melted shortening or vegetable oil
1/4 cup powdered skim milk
1/2 cup whole milk
2 teaspoons salt
2-3/4 cups white flour
1 package active dry yeast

Mix the above ingredients in a large bowl and add the starter with coffee and caraway. Cover the bowl and let the dough rise until it doubles. Then knead on a lightly floured surface and shape into two round loaves on a baking sheet.

Let rise until double again, and bake at 350°F. for half an hour or more, or until loaves sound hollow when rapped with a spoon.

~~~~~~

SHEEPHERDER BREAD

1-1/2 cups sourdough starter
4 cups flour
2 tablespoons sugar
2 tablespoons melted shortening
1 teaspoon salt
1/4 teaspoon baking soda

Sift all of the dry ingredients into a large bowl and dig a well in the center. Add the sourdough starter.

Blend the dry mix into the starter from the edges with enough flour to knead until smooth and shiny. Place in greased bowl, cover with a towel, and let rise until doubled in size. Then shape into two loaves and place in greased bread pans. Bake at 375°F. about 40 minutes or until bread sounds hollow when rapped with a spoon.

SOURDOUGH CAMP BREAD

This bread is for the rough-and-ready outdoorsman and is simple to make.

4 cups of sourdough starter
1 tablespoon of melted shortening or vegetable oil
1 cup flour
1 teaspoon baking powder

Add shortening, flour and baking powder to the starter. Keep adding flour until no more can be absorbed. Form into loaves. Put in a greased bowl, cover with a towel and allow to stand in a warm place until loaves have doubled in size. Shape into two loaves and place in oiled bread pans. Bake at 350°F. about 40 minutes or until bread sounds hollow when rapped with a spoon.

TRAPPER'S SOURDOUGH BREAD

2 cups sourdough starter
2 tablespoons sugar
4 cups flour
1 teaspoon salt
2 tablespoons shortening or vegetable oil

Mix the flour, salt, and sugar and scoop a hollow in it. Pour in the melted shortening and blend it with the sourdough starter inside the hollow.

Then mix into a soft batter. Add flour if too moist; or milk or water if too dry. Knead well but don't let the gases escape. Bang it around as fast as possible and break off into two loaf-sized chunks. Let rise until doubled in size, punch down, then place in greased bread pans. Preheat oven to 425°F. and bake for 15 minutes at this heat. Turn heat down to 350°F. and finish baking for for about an hour. Baking should result in doubling the size again, and the loaves should turn out crispy brown.

BOSTON BROWN BREAD

1 cup corn meal
1 cup rye flour
1 cup graham flour
1 teaspoon soda
4 teaspoons baking powder
1 teaspoon salt
3/4 cup molasses
2 cups sour milk or buttermilk
2 cups sweet milk

Mix the dry ingredients and add the molasses and the milk. Beat the mixture thoroughly, and pour into oiled molds until they are about 3/4 full. Cover loosely to keep out the moisture, and steam for 3 1/2 hours. Remove the covers and bake the bread in oven heated to 350°F. for 10 minutes to dry off.

PIONEER BREAD

2/3 cup yellow cornmeal
1/2 cup packed brown sugar
2 teaspoons salt
2 cups boiling water
1/4 cup olive oil
2 packages active dry yeast
1/2 cup very warm water (110°F. to 115°F.)
3/4 cup stirred whole-wheat flour
1/2 cup stirred rye flour
4-1/4 to 4-1/2 cups unsifted all-purpose flour

Grease two 8-1/2 x 4-1/2 x 2-1/2 inch loaf pan and sprinkle each with 1 tablespoon cornmeal.

In a large bowl, thoroughly combine remaining cornmeal, brown sugar, salt, 2 cups boiling water and shortening. Let cool to lukewarm, about 30 minutes.

Soften yeast in 1/2 cup very warm water; stir into cornmeal mixture. For stirred flour, stir the flour gently with a spoon to lighten before measuring. Add whole-wheat and rye flours; mix well. Stir in enough all-purpose flour to make a moderately stiff dough.

Turn dough out onto a floured board and knead until smooth, 6 to 8 minutes. Return dough to a greased bowl, cover, set in a warm place and let rise until doubled in bulk about 50 to 60 minutes.

Divide dough in half, let rest 5 minutes. Shape dough into 2 loaves. Place into prepared loaf pans. Cover and let rise for about 30 to 40 minutes.

Bake in a preheated 375°F. oven for 45 minutes or until loaves sound hollow when rapped with a spoon. Turn out of pans; cool on rack. Makes two loaves.

SOURDOUGH PANCAKES

CORNMEAL STARTER
1 cup unbleached flour
1 cup cornmeal
2 tablespoons sugar
water

Mix unbleached flour, cornmeal, sugar, and enough water to make a medium batter. Cover with a small towel and set in a warm place. This should start to ferment in about 5 hours. When you can smell the delightful aroma, put the starter in a cool place. It will be ready to use the next day.

PANCAKE BATTER
2 cups flour
1 cup cornmeal
1/3 cup sugar
water
1 teaspoon baking soda
3 eggs
1 cup canned milk
1 teaspoon baking soda
1/3 teaspoon salt

Beginning the night before, mix flour, cornmeal, sugar, and enough water to make a batter. Add this right into your starter crock. Next morning the starter should be fermenting at a low level, so pour out an amount equal to what you added the night before into a large bowl. Put the remaining starter back in storage and proceed with the batter. To this add eggs, canned milk, water, soda, and salt.. Beat hard. If you like thin pancakes—and western pancakes are generally thin—add water to make a thin batter. For authentic sour flavor--go easy on the soda, or leave out the soda altogether. Cook on a heavy iron griddle, using a little vegetable oil.

If you prefer regular white flour pancakes, leave out the cornmeal after the original fermentation of sourdough. Use all white flour instead. Or you can use a mixture of white flour and buckwheat or white flour and farina, giving different flavors and textures. It is best to make a thin gruel of the farina if it is used.

BOLILLOS

These easy-to-do traditional Mexican hard rolls go great with any meal. They stay fresh in the freezer for up to three months.

> 1 package active dry yeast
> 2 teaspoons sugar
> 1-3/4 cups warm water (105°F. to 115°F.)
> 1 teaspoon salt
> 6 cups sifted all-purpose flour

Stir yeast and sugar together, then dissolve in warm water. Add the salt, then the flour, 2 cups at a time, beating well after each addition. After adding the fifth cup of flour, add flour slowly until the dough becomes too stiff to handle.

Turn out onto a lightly floured board and knead until smooth. Place in a lightly oiled bowl, being sure to oil the top of the bread, then cover with a sheet of wax paper and a towel.

Let rise in a warm place free of drafts until doubled in bulk. When dough is doubled, punch down and allow to double again.

Form into long slender rolls, twisting each end. You can roll the dough into very long ropes about 2 inches in diameter and cut off 3 to 4 inch pieces of dough, twisting each end. Authentic Mexican-style rolls, should be rather flat with twisted ends. Lay rolls about 2 inches apart on a lightly floured baking sheet.

Now slash the top of each roll with a sharp knife. Cover with a towel and again allow to double in bulk. When nearly doubled, preheat oven to 400°F. and lightly oil the tops of the rolls.

Bake for 30 to 40 minutes, until lightly browned. Serve piping hot with lots of butter. Makes 3 dozen rolls.

BLUE CORN BREAD

1-1/2 cups blue cornmeal
2 teaspoons baking powder
3 tablespoons sugar
3-1/4 cup milk
1 large egg, beaten
3 tablespoons bacon fat or vegetable oil
1 small can green chilies, chopped

Combine first three ingredients. Mix remaining ingredients in separate bowl.

Add liquid mix to dry ingredients and mix thoroughly. Pour into greased baking pan and bake in preheated oven at 350° for 30 minutes or until toothpick comes out clean. Makes about 4 servings.

SOUR MILK BISCUITS

2 cups flour
1 teaspoon salt
2 teaspoon baking powder
1/2 teaspoon soda
2 tablespoons lard or shortening
1 cup sour milk or buttermilk

Sift dry ingredients into mixing bowl. Mix in lard or shortening with finger tips.

To make sour milk you can put 1 tablespoon of white cider vinegar into a 1 cup measuring cup, then fill with milk. Let stand at room temperature for an hour or so. Add sour milk or buttermilk. Mix into a soft and spongy dough. Turn out onto a lightly floured board, roll 1/2 inch thick, and cut into biscuit circles. Lightly flour shallow pan or cookie sheet, place biscuits not too close together, and bake for 12 minutes. Makes 1-1/2 dozen.

CORN DOUGHGODS

Doughgods were devised by pioneers with no provisions but flour and salt. Flour, water, and salt were baked on a griddle, but without leavening they came out barely chewable. In the winter, when camped near the snow-line, the flour dough would be buried in a snowbank and when almost frozen, mixed with a good measure of snow. The snow crystals would bake out leaving small holes similar to a leavening agent such as baking powder. Pounded, dried berries would sometimes be added to help vary the taste of baked flour, which was a trick learned from the Indians. This variation of Doughgods is much more tasty and was sometimes used as a dessert.

1 quart flour
4 tablespoons baking powder
1 quart cornmeal
2 cups shortening
1 tablespoon salt
1 cup sugar, optional
water

Melt the shortening in a heavy skillet. Dip out a cupful of this to cool and leave the rest in the pan, hot. Mix cooled oil, flour, cornmeal, salt, and baking powder. The sugar is optional. Add water and stir to make a heavy batter.

Spoon this immediately into the hot oil, which should be in sufficient quantity to bubble up, halfway floating the Doughgods. Turn them over when brown.

In the Old West, cooks would have used bacon and salt pork to make the necessary oil and would have served the cooked bacon or salt pork with the Doughgods.

For a luxury touch, the Corn Doughgods may be dipped in sugar and cinnamon as a dessert.

MOYETTES

5 cups sifted all-purpose flour
2 cups sugar
pinch of salt
3 tablespoons butter or vegetable oil
1 package active dry yeast
1 cup warm water
1 egg, slightly beaten
2 teaspoons anise extract or 1/4 cup anis seeds
1/2 cup melted butter or margarine
2 teaspoons ground cinnamon

Sift together flour, 1 cup sugar and salt. Mix in butter until the mixture resembles coarse meal. If using oil, stir oil into liquid ingredients after adding the egg.

Dissolve yeast in warm water (use 2 packages to shorten time), stir vigorously, and allow to ferment for 10 minutes. Then add the egg and anise extract or anis seeds.

Add a small amount of the flour mixture to the yeast and beat until thoroughly blended. Let stand for a few minutes, or until dough becomes light and airy.

Add the rest of the flour mixture, adding more flour if necessary to make a stiff dough. Knead on a lightly floured board until smooth. Oil the top of the dough, cover with wax paper and let it rise until doubled. When the bread has risen, punch it down, and let it rise until doubled again.

Knead the dough slightly, then form into balls the size of an orange. With a rolling pin, flatten to 1/2 to 3/4 inch thick. Prepare a topping by mixing together the melted butter, remaining 1 cup sugar and the cinnamon. Spread topping on all sides of the rolls.

Let rolls rise until light and about doubled in size. When nearly doubled, preheat oven to 400°F. Bake for 20 to 25 minutes, or until golden. Makes 8 to 10 small loaves. To serve, slice thinly, butter and arrange slices on a platter.

JALAPEÑO SPOONBREAD

*The heat of jalapeño chilies combines with cumin, corn,
and Cheddar cheese to give this spoonable, pudding-like
bread a fiery flavor.*

2 eggs
2 cans (about 1 pound. each) cream-style corn
1 small onion, finely chopped
1 can (2-1/4 oz.) sliced ripe olives, drained
1/3 cup vegetable oil
*4 to 7 jalapeño chilies, stemmed, seeded,
and finely chopped*
1 teaspoon each garlic salt and baking powder
1/2 teaspoon ground cumin
3/4 cup yellow cornmeal
2 cups (8 ounces) shredded Cheddar cheese

In a large bowl, beat eggs; add corn, onion, olives, oil,
and chilies. Set aside. In another bowl, combine garlic
salt, baking powder, cumin, and cornmeal. Add to egg
mixture with 1 cup of the cheese. Stir to blend thoroughly.

Pour batter into a well-greased 9-inch cast-iron frying
pan or 9-inch square baking pan. Scatter remaining 1
cup cheese over top.

Bake in a 350°F. oven until golden brown (about 40 to
50 minutes). Spoon out of pan. Makes 6 servings.

NAVAJO FRY BREAD

This traditional version of Indian bread also makes a great taco and is good when served with most chile dishes.

lard or vegetable oil
2 cups all-purpose flour, unsifted
4 teaspoons baking powder
1 teaspoon salt
2/3 cup warm water or more
cornmeal

Put enough melted lard or oil in a deep-fryer to reach a depth of 2 to 3 inches. Heat lard or oil (lard is traditional) to 400°F.

Combine flour, baking powder and salt. Add 1/2 cup warm water and continue adding water to reach the consistency of bread dough; more water may be needed.

Tear off balls of dough. Roll out balls on a board lightly dusted with cornmeal or flour until each is 1/4 inch thick.

Punch a hole in the center of each piece; the hole is a traditional mark of fry bread and comes from the Navajo custom of sticking a branch into the bread and lowering it into the hot oil.

Fry one bread at a time, turning each as soon as it becomes golden. Drain on absorbent paper towel and serve hot with honey or dusted with powdered sugar. Makes one dozen pieces.

Santa Fe Bob sez:

Fry Bread was a staple of the Navajo diet. The Indians made it in various ways, sometimes using all cornmeal instead of wheat flour and sometimes adding wild berries, seeds or nuts during the summer to add variety. The Navajo take this bread with them while out herding sheep and goats.

Cooks of the Old West who journeyed through the Southwest, stole the recipe and found ways to incorporate it into their menus. It's a popular attraction at fairs and outdoor events in New Mexico. It's not unusual to see people lined up for almost a block to wait their turn to get some freshly made fry bread.

Mexican Sopaipillas ("sofa pillows") were another recipe appropriated by Old West cooks. An immediate favorite of all who tried them, these hollow fried breads originated in Old Town, Albuquerque, NM, about 300 years ago. They are traditionally dusted with cinnamon and sugar and served as a dessert, but can be served as a hot main course with beans and chile.

SOPAIPILLAS

4 cups sifted all-purpose flour
1-1/2 teaspoons salt
1 teaspoon baking powder
1 tablespoon lard, butter or margarine
1 package active dry yeast (optional)
1/4 cup warm water (105°F. to 115°F.)
1-1/4 cups scalded milk
approximately 1 quart lard or cooking oil

Combine dry ingredients and mix in 1 tablespoon lard, butter or margarine. Dissolve yeast in the water. Add yeast to scalded milk, cooled to room temperature. If not using yeast, use 1-1/2 cups milk and omit the 1/4 cup warm water.

Make a well in the center of dry ingredients. Add about 1-1/4 cups liquid to dry ingredients and work into dough. Add more liquid until dough is firm and springy and holds its shape, similar to a yeast dough.

Knead dough 15 to 20 times, then invert the bowl over the dough and set aside for approximately 10 minutes. Heat 1 quart lard or oil to 420°F. in a deep-fryer.

Roll one fourth of the dough to 1/4-inch thickness or slightly thinner, then cut into squares or triangles. Do not reroll any of the dough. Cover the cut dough with a towel as you fry the sopaipillas, a few at a time, in the hot fat. They should puff up and become hollow very soon after being dropped into the fat. To assure puffing, slightly stretch each piece of dough before lowering it into the fat, then place the rolled or top side of dough into the fat first, so it will be the bottom side. Hold each piece of dough down in the fat until it puffs. Drain sopaipillas on absorbent paper towel.

Sopaipillas may be dusted with a sugar-cinnamon mixture and are especially good with honey. Stuff hot large sopaipillas with refried beans, chile con carne, chopped onion, grated cheese and lettuce or guacamole for a main dish.

Sopaipillas can be frozen for up to three months. To

serve, heat in a foil packet in a 350°F. oven for about 15 minutes. Just before serving, open the foil so that the sopaipillas will dry out on the outside. Makes 4 dozen.

RHUBARB BREAD

1-1/2 cups brown sugar
2/3 cup butter, softened
1 egg, beaten
1 cup sour milk (or buttermilk)
2-1/2 cups flour
1 teaspoon. soda
1/2 teaspoon salt
1-1/2 cups raw rhubarb, diced
1/2 cups walnuts, chopped

Cream brown sugar and butter together until fluffy. Stir in egg, sour milk, and vanilla.

In a separate bowl sift together dry ingredients and stir into first mixture. Mix well. Stir in rhubarb and nuts.

Pour batter into small greased loaf pans. Bake in 325° F. oven 35-40 minutes.

TORTILLAS

4 cups blue or yellow cornmeal
2 teaspoons salt
2 teaspoons baking powder
1/2 teaspoon sugar (creates a browner bubbled surface)
4 tablespoons lard or butter
1-1/2 cups warm water or milk

Combine flour, salt, baking powder in a large mixing bowl, blending thoroughly. Work in lard or butter with a pastry blender or your fingers.

Add water or milk gradually until dough is stiff but not sticky. Knead the dough 15 to 20 times and let stand for 10 minutes.

Pull off a small piece of dough about the size of a egg and roll it into a flat round of 6 inches in diameter and 1/8-inch thick.

Heat a large cast iron griddle or stove lid and drop tortillas one at a time onto griddle. Brown each side until it has light brown flecks. Place tortillas in a tea towel or special tortilla server to remain warm until serving. They will stay warm for at least 15 minutes. Makes 8 to 12 tortillas.

NOTE: White or wheat flour may be substituted for cornmeal. Be sure to use lard or butter only as vegetable shortening tends to make tough tortillas.

WILD SAGE BREAD

1 package dry yeast
1 cup cottage cheese
1 egg
1 tablespoon lard or other shortening, melted
1 tablespoon sugar
2 teaspoon crushed dried wild sage
1 teaspoon salt
1/4 teaspoon baking soda
1/4 cup lukewarm water
2-1/2 cups flour

Mix dry ingredients together. Dissolve yeast in warm water. Beat together egg and cheese until smooth. Add melted shortening and yeast.

Combine all ingredients in a large mixing bowl, adding flour mixture in small amounts and blending thoroughly after each addition. Form a stiff dough. Cover dough with a tea towel and allow to rise in a warm place for an hour or until dough has doubled in size.

After dough has doubled, punch dough down and knead for one minute. Place dough in a well-greased loaf or casserole pan. Cover and allow to rise again for 40 minutes. Bake in a preheated 350°F. oven for 50 minutes or until bread sounds hollow when tapped with a spoon. Makes 1 loaf.

HARDTACK

In the Old West, hardtack was the simplest of all non-perishable meals and was conveniently carried by cowboys in their saddlebags. Until as recently as World War I it was the staple food of traveling armies, who called it "sheet-iron," "tooth-dullers," "crown-breakers," and other names best forgotten. It was eaten dry only in emergencies, and then was more sucked on than chewed. Dipped in hot coffee, hardtack becomes edible. Soak it well in water and fry in salt pork fat and you've got a hearty meal on the trail.

All modern crackers are dimpled in the manner of hardtack, which was pricked with nail holes to keep it compact and breakable.

3-1/4 cups unbleached, all-purpose flour
3 teaspoons salt
water

Preheat the oven to 375°F. In the bowl mix 3 cups of flour with the salt. Add 1 cup of tap water and stir until it becomes too difficult. Knead dough in bowl with hand, adding more flour to make it very dry.

Press, pull, and roll the dough into a rectangle that can be divided into 3-inch squares of 1/2-inch thickness.

Use a table knife to cut dough into squares. Holding each square in hand, punch 16 holes through it with an eight-penny nail, being careful not to hurt yourself.

Place dough squares on ungreased baking sheets and bake for 30 minutes, until crisp and lightly browned. Cool before storing in a closed container. Makes 16 pieces.

REAL GINGERBREAD

2 cups cake flour
2 teaspoons baking powder
1/2 teaspoon soda
1/2 teaspoon salt
2 teaspoons ginger
1-1/2 teaspoons cinnamon
1/4 teaspoon ground cloves
1/4 teaspoon nutmeg
1 stick butter or margarine
1/2 cup dark brown sugar
2 eggs, beaten
1 cup buttermilk
1 cup molasses

Sift dry ingredients into a large mixing bowl. In a separate bowl cream sugar and butter. Beat in eggs, then buttermilk, then molasses.

Gradually stir liquid mixture into the bowl of dry ingredients. Beat thoroughly. Pour into greased 8 x 12 baking pan. Bake in moderate (350°F.) oven 30-35 minutes.

SHREDDED WHEAT BREAD

3/4 cup shredded wheat biscuits (cereal)
3 teaspoons salt
3/4 cup grapenuts (cereal)
2 cups boiling water
1/2 cup sorghum molasses
2 cups scalded milk
1/2 cup shortening
2 packages dry yeast
1/2 cup brown sugar
8 cups all-purpose flour

In a large saucepan combine shredded wheat biscuits (crumbled), grapenuts, sorghum, shortening, brown sugar and salt. Stir in boiling water. Let stand 10 minutes. Allow scalded milk to cool to lukewarm and stir in yeast until it's dissolved. Stir milk-yeast into shredded wheat mixture. Gradually add flour until dough becomes stiff.

Turn out onto a lightly floured surface and knead 8-10 minutes. Place in greased bowl in a warm location and let rise to double in bulk. Punch down and shape into three loaves. Place in greased 9 x 5 loaf pans and let rise to tops of pans. Bake in moderate (350° F.) oven 35-40 minutes.

SWEDISH CRACKERS

These traditional soft crackers were prepared at Christmastime and made their way into the Old West with settlers of Scandinavian descent.

Baker's ammonia is a leavening agent still used in holiday baking by cooks of Scandinavian and German heritage. It is a salt called ammonium carbonate that can be found in some pharmacies and specialty food stores. With a mallet, crush coarse salts before using in a cloth

All ammonia salts, coarse or fine, attract moisture and should be bought and kept in tight containers.

1/4 cup milk
.35 ounce fine Ammonium carbonate
1/2 cup shortening or margarine
1-1/2 cups sugar
2 eggs, beaten
2 teaspoons lemon extract
3 to 4 cups unbleached all-purpose flour

Scald milk in a small saucepan. Put the ammonium carbonate in small bowl, pour the hot milk over it, and cover bowl with a plate or lid as the mixture foams up. Let this mixture cool while oiling two large baking sheets. Blend shortening and sugar in a large mixing bowl. Beat into this the eggs, lemon extract, remaining 1/2 cup milk, and 2 cups of flour. Stir in the cooled milk mixture (no longer foamy) and another cup of flour to make a stiff batter. Add more flour, 2 cups at a time, until the dough is firm enough to roll out.

Turn out onto a lightly floured surface and roll dough into a rectangle about 10 inches by 23 inches by 1/4 inch. With a floured knife, cut the dough into 2-1/2 inch squares, about 36 in all.

Preheat the oven to 350°F. Place squares on the baking sheets so they are not touching and prick them with a fork to make a design. Bake crackers in a moderate oven until they are lightly tanned, 10 to 15 minutes. Remove from pans to cool. Makes about 3 dozen crackers.

PAPER BREAD

1/4 cup yellow or blue cornmeal for tortillas
3/4 teaspoon of salt
8 cups of water
1/4 cup cornstarch
lard or vegetable shortening

In a 3 to 4 quart pan, combine cornmeal and salt. Blend in 7 cups water until smooth. Bring to a boil over high heat, stirring with a long spoon being careful of spatters. Reduce heat to low and simmer, uncovered, for 15 minutes; stirring occasionally.

Mix 1 cup of water with cornstarch. Blend into the cornmeal mixture and return to a boil. Cook for 1 minute, stirring. Remove from heat.

Heat an electric griddle to 350° (or place a regular griddle over medium heat; it's ready when a drop of water dances). To prevent spatters, you can make a barrier of foil on 3 sides of griddle.

Coat griddle with lard or solid vegetable shortening. Pour 1/4 to 1/2 cup of corn gruel onto griddle (watch out for hot spatters). With a long, flexible spatula, gently guide liquid to form a rectangle, about 8 by 10 inches. Cook until bread is dry and pulls from griddle (about 5 minutes). With dry spatula and fingers, gently lift bread from griddle.

Grease griddle and cook another sheet of paper bread; when half dry, lay cooked sheet of paper bread directly on top (if cooked bread breaks, use pieces). Continue to cook until bread pulls from griddle (about 15 more minutes) to make a doublethick piece of bread. Loosely fold hot sheets (bread will break).

Repeat procedure to make each piece of bread. Serve at room temperature; or let cool, then store airtight at room temperature for up to 1 week. Makes 6 to 8 pieces.

Desserts

The Old West was a world without frozen pies and cakes, packaged ice cream, and wrapped candy bars. The confections we take for granted require a large and steady supply of sugar. White cane sugar, was initially a precious item on the frontier, but changes came soon. In Europe, sugar was being extracted from sugar beets. In England and America, factories were being built that would clarify sugar by fast new methods. "Penny candies" such as peppermint sticks, horehound drops, ribbon candies, and valentine hearts soon became a regular treat from the general store.

As the second half of the 1800's gave rise to penny candy, it also gave rise—quite literally—to cakes as home confections. When cooking was done in a fireplace, steamed puddings were the usual sweet served with dinner. Since egg whites were required to make batter rise, light cakes were enjoyed only by those who could afford the eggs and the labor to beat them.

The introduction of cookstoves with ovens made the popularization of the dessert pie possible. The use of another cake leaven, a chemical called saleratus that reacts with the acid of sour milk or cream to produce a gas, also became popular in home baking. By the 1860's, someone invented baking soda by combining saleratus with a dry acid (cream of tartar). That made cake baking practically instantaneous and gave birth to the American layer cake.

By and large, Old West desserts were dominated by

flour and sugar since those dry staple goods were a constant on the frontier. Flavorings such as chocolate and fruit occasionally complimented the primary ingredients. The wild berries that ripened, the fruit that matured, and the extracts that could be bought from the general store were added and combined to make good, sturdy desserts. Pioneers of German and Czech descent made the most desserts, using recipes from the old country modified to utilize available ingredients. Farm wives who had an abundance of eggs perfected meringue pies and angel food cakes.

Most Southwest-style meals ended with simple desserts to contrast the rich spiciness of the main dishes. Fruits and various custards were popular traditional choices. Cookies were frequently served alongside to add to texture and flavor.

Fresh fruit assortments of almost any combination were popular. Contemporary favorites include mango slices generously splashed with fresh lime juice and garnished with pomegranate seeds, blueberries or other berries. Guava jelly bar candy available in Mexican and Southwestern delicacy shops is excellent cut into bite-size pieces and served with chunks of Monterey Jack cheese. Desserts made with at least three types of melon (such as watermelon, honeydew and cantaloupe) are popular and can be marinated in tequila for a special touch.

APPLE DENVER PIE

6 tart apples
1 tablespoon flour
2 tablespoons butter
1 teaspoon nutmeg
2 cups water
1 cup white sugar
1/2 cup brown sugar

Wash, peel, and core apples; place cores and peelings in saucepan with 2 cups of water and boil down until one cup of juice is left. Strain; add sugar, flour, nutmeg, and butter. Place saucepan on stove and boil until it is a little thick, then cool. Slice apples into crust; then pour the thickened juice over apples; place top crust on and vent. Dampen pie with a little cold water and sprinkle with a little white sugar. Bake at 240°F. until apples are done and the crust is nice and brown.

PIE CRUST

1-1/2 cups flour
1/4 teaspoon baking powder
1/2 teaspoon salt
1/3 cup shortening

Sift together flour, salt, and baking soda. Spoon the shortening into the flour mixture and blend with fingers (not warm palms) until uniformly coarse. Continue to toss while adding enough ice cold water (about 3 tablespoons) to make a very stiff dough. Press the dough into a ball and chill in the refrigerator while preparing the filling. Roll out thin on a pastry surface lightly dusted with flour and fold over, and roll again. Do this several times, dusting lightly with flour each time. The more folds, the flakier the crust. Butter the pie pan. Transfer the dough by folding it in quarters, placing in a pan, and unfolding. Trim with knife around edge and pinch for fluted edge. This makes one 9-inch shell. Double the recipe for a two-crust pie.

BOILED APPLE DUMPLINGS

1 cup sour milk
1 teaspoon salt
1/4 teaspoon soda
1 tablespoon lard or margarine
1 teaspoon baking powder
flour
2 cups of applesauce
sugar and cinnamon to taste

Mix milk, melted lard, soda, salt, and baking powder. To this add enough flour to make a stiff dough. Roll on floured board about 1/4 inch thick. Cut in 4 inch squares. Put 3 tablespoons applesauce seasoned to taste with sugar and cinnamon on each square. Fold over dough and press edges together. Put each dumpling into its own muslin sack. Drop into kettle of boiling water in which there is a rack. Boil 30 minutes. Serve with cream or hard sauce.

HARD SAUCE FOR APPLE DUMPLINGS

1/2 cup butter or margarine
2 teaspoons vanilla
1/4 cup hot canned milk
2 cups powdered sugar
pinch of salt

Mix together canned milk and sugar, vanilla, and salt. Shape in a cake 1 inch thick and chill. Cut in slices and serve on hot dumplings.

BURNT SUGAR ANGEL FOOD CAKE

1 pint flour
1-1/3 pint sugar
15 egg whites
1/4 teaspoon salt
1 teaspoon Cream of Tartar
1 teaspoon vanilla
2 tablespoons burnt sugar

Sift flour, sugar, and salt 6 times together. Beat egg whites until stiff. When partly beaten, add cream of tartar. Finish beating. Add vanilla and burnt sugar. Stir flour and sugar in very slowly. Bake in ungreased pan 1-1/4 hours in a very low oven (350°F.). Add a little burnt sugar can also be added to the icing.

DOUGHNUTS

1 cup sugar
1 cup sour milk
3 teaspoons fat or margarine
2 eggs
1 teaspoon soda, dissolved
1/2 teaspoons cinnamon
4 cups flour

Sprinkle enough flour to roll out dough. After cutting, let rise 30 minutes before dropping in hot fat.

COWBOY DRIED APPLE PIE

pie crust dough (see Apple Denver Pie)
2 cups cooked dried apples
1 tablespoon butter
1 cup cooked raisins
1 tablespoon vinegar
3/4 cup brown sugar
1 teaspoon cinnamon

Mix all ingredients in a bowl. In place of vinegar, you may use 2 tablespoons of lemon juice with the grated rind of one small orange. Pour mixture into pie crust, then place top crust and vent. Moisten top with a little milk and sprinkle with sugar. Bake at 240°F. until filling is bubbling and the crust is nice and brown.

SCOTCH SHORT BREAD

3-1/2 cups sifted flour
1/2 cup sugar
1 cup butter
1/4 teaspoon salt

Sift together flour, salt and sugar on a cutting board. Work butter into dry ingredients, kneading with your palm, until it is an even mixture. Make the dough into a ball and roll out about 3/4 of an inch thick. Place in a pan with high sides to prevent the short bread from browning too quickly around the edges, and prick the surface with a fork. Bake in a very moderate oven, 300°F., for 35 minutes. Allow the short bread to stand an hour or two before serving so that it becomes crisp and thoroughly set, then slice into serving pieces.

FRIED PEACH PIE

Fried Peach Pie is a great outdoor treat because it can be made without an oven or a dutch oven.

pie crust dough (see recipe with Denver Apple Pie)
4 cups sugar
1 pound dried peaches
3 cups water
1 teaspoon nutmeg
1/2 cup flour

Chop the peaches to about 1/2-inch pieces and boil with sugar and grated nutmeg. The 3 cups of water is an approximation because dried peaches vary greatly in water content. Boil gently until peaches plump, and set aside to cool.

Make a double pie crust dough, using less (only 1/2 cup) shortening. Roll out and cut into circles approximately 8 inches across. Place a circle of dough on a small mixing bowl and push the middle down an inch or so. Spoon in 1/2 cup of fruit—or enough to fill the depression. Place a second circle of dough on top. Pinch the edges together and form a pastry shell. Using a fork, puncture 3 or 4 steam vents along the seam on either side. Pan fry in about a tablespoon of oil, or bake until the crust is brittle and caramelized peach juice has formed.

GINGER CREAMS

1/2 cup shortening
1 cup sugar
1 egg
1 cup molasses
4 cups flour
1/2 teaspoon salt
1 teaspoon nutmeg
2 teaspoons ginger
1 teaspoon cloves
1 teaspoon cinnamon
1 cup hot water
2 teaspoons soda

Mix shortening and sugar. Add egg, molasses, and hot water to which soda has been added. Sift the remaining dry ingredients together and add to the liquid mixture. Drop by teaspoonful onto an oiled cookie sheet. Bake until brown at 375°F.

HASTY PUDDING

1/2 cup sugar
2/3 cup flour
nutmeg
heavy cream

Put two cups of hot water in the top of a double boiler. Stir in 1/4 teaspoon salt and 1/2 cup of sugar. When it comes to a boil, add 2/3 cups of flour a little at a time, and whip with a whisk while cooking. Don't overblend, the pudding should look a little like tapioca. Cook two minutes. Serve into individual bowls and sprinkle with nutmeg. Top with heavy cream.

MOLASSES PIE

2 cups sorghum molasses
1/2 cup sugar
1/2 cup water
5 eggs
pinch of salt
1 teaspoon corn starch
pinch of soda
1 teaspoon butter
dash of nutmeg

Save the whites of 2 eggs for meringue. Beat 3 eggs and 2 yolks. Stir in 2 cups of molasses, sugar, water, and salt. Pour into top of double boiler, add corn starch; then place over hot water and stir while cooking. Cook until quite thick. Stir in soda, butter, nutmeg. Set aside to cool while baking a large, deep-crust pie shell. When the filling is cool, pour into pie shell. Make meringue and pile on top of pie; place in oven until light brown. This makes a large pie.

BAKELESS CAKE

1/2 cup butter
1 cup sugar
1 egg yolk
1 large can crushed pineapple
1 cup chopped nuts
3 tablespoons cream
1 package vanilla wafers

Put a layer of vanilla wafers in a shallow pan. Mix the rest of the ingredients together. Spread layer of filling on wafers. Do this until 3 layers of wafers and 2 of filling are completed. Let set up for 4 hours in the refrigerator. Serve with whipped cream.

SODA CRACKER PIE

3 egg whites
1 cup sugar
16 soda crackers
1/4 teaspoon baking powder
1/2 cup nut meats
1 teaspoons vanilla

Beat egg whites until stiff. Add 1 cup sugar gradually, then add the soda crackers which have been rolled fine, and combined with the baking powder. Last, add nut meats and vanilla. Spread in buttered 9-inch pie plate and bake 325°F. oven for 30 minutes. When cold, cover with a layer of fresh strawberries or bananas. Top with sweetened whipped cream. Chill 2 hours before serving.

SOUR CREAM RAISIN PIE

1 cup sour cream
2/3 cup raisins
1 scant cup sugar
1/2 teaspoon cinnamon
1/4 teaspoon cloves
1 teaspoon salt
3 egg yolks and 1 white

Mix cream and raisins together in a saucepan over low heat. In a bowl, beat together 3 egg yolks and 1 white. Add sugar, spice, salt; beat well. Add egg mixture to the cream and raisins and cook, stirring constantly, as it burns easily.

Pour into a baked pie shell. Cover with a meringue made with 2 egg whites. When pie has cooled, brown in the oven to a light brown.

SHEEP SHEARER'S DELIGHT
OR DIRTY GEORGE

Unlike cowboys on the trail, sheep shearers had a ready source of milk and often robbed a lamb of its next meal while the mother ewe was being sheared. This authentic bread pudding was a favorite.

When made with canned milk, Sheep Shearer's Delight went by the name of Dirty George. But it is not known-whether the name was in honor of the cook or because of the blotchy, gray-brown appearance of the dish.

In winter, some cooks served Dirty George as a treat with a topping of snow-whipped canned milk. They would pour a can of sweetened condensed milk into a crockery bowl and set outside when the temperature was below zero (you can use your freezer and blender-crushed ice). When the milk was bladed with ice, they stirred in a handful of loose, crisp snow and beat until light. An excellent flavoring for this may be made by boiling sweetened leftover coffee until thick and adding a few drops of vanilla then adding to the topping.

1 loaf bread, sliced
1/2 cup molasses
butter or margarine to spread
1/2 cup corn syrup
1 quart sheep's milk, whole milk or condensed milk

Spread the sliced bread with butter on both sides, arrange in a pan, and cover with a mixture of milk, molasses, and syrup. Bake in a slow oven about 2 hours, stirring gently from time to time and adding milk if needed. Serve with cold milk to which a few drops of vanilla have been added.

Santa Fe Bob Sez:

Until only recently people were ignorant of the health risks of high-fat foods. Some of these recipes originally called for lard or suet. You can substitute margarine or shortening, but the flavor will be a little different.

Many authentic Old West recipes like Son-of-a-Gun in a Sack, Vinegar Pie and Hasty Pudding used only the simplest ingredients available on the trail.

Visitors at camps where Vinegar Pie was made asked for the recipe and were amazed to hear that there was nothing in the filling except suet, sugar, water, and vinegar. They thought there must be a secret ingredient.

The wonderful flavor came from the sugar, bubbling and caramelizing through holes in the crust, and from the vinegar which substituted for fruit acid. And if the cook had a few leftover dried peaches, he might cut them up and mix them in to heighten the illusion of fruit in his Vinegar Pie. Indeed, many favorite Old West desserts were created by ingenious cooks looking to top off a hearty meal.

SON-OF-A-GUN IN A SACK

2 cups flour
1 cup canned milk
1 cup raisins
1 tablespoon soda
1 teaspoon cinnamon
1 teaspoon nutmeg
1 cup bread crumbs
1 cup ground suet
1 cup molasses
1 teaspoon salt
1 teaspoon cloves

Dissolve soda in molasses. Combine flour, bread crumbs, salt and spices. Then mix these dry ingredients with the suet, raisins, molasses, nuts, and canned milk. Mix well, pour into a cloth sack and tie with a string. Then boil in water for 2 hours. Remove from sack and serve in bowls topped with Foamy Sauce (recipe follows).

FOAMY SAUCE

1/2 cup butter
1 cup confectioner's sugar
1 egg
2 tablespoons hot water
1 teaspoon vanilla

Cream butter and sugar together. Add the well-beaten egg and the hot water until the mixture thickens, beating continuously. Add vanilla and serve on top of Son-of-a-Gun in a Sack.

VINEGAR PIE

pastry dough (use recipe with Denver Apple Pie)
1/2 cup vinegar
1/2 pound suet
flour as needed
1 cup water
1 cup sugar
dried peaches, optional

Chop the suet and fry out. Discard the cracklings. Add water and bring to a boil. Add the vinegar. Stir in flour slowly, creaming to form a paste. Add sugar and pour into a dough-lined pie tin. Add dried peaches if available.

Cover with dough, cut numerous openings for escaping steam, sprinkle sugar over the top, and bake until the crust is crisp and brown. The result is surprisingly like a fruit pie.

NAVAJO CAKE

6 cups water
4 cups cooked blue corn meal
2 cups cooked yellow corn meal
1/2 cup raisins
1 cup sprouted wheat
1/2 cup brown sugar

Bring water to a boil in a large heavy saucepan. Add blue cornmeal, yellow cornmeal, raisins, sprouted wheat, and brown sugar, stirring constantly over low heat.

Blend until all ingredients are thoroughly mixed. Pour mixture into a large baking pan or casserole and cover with foil. Bake in a preheated 250°F. oven for 4 hours or until cake is firm. Makes 8 servings.

WALNUT HONEY CAKE

1 pound shelled walnuts (ground finely)
12 slices Zwieback toast
1 pound powdered sugar
1 teaspoon each of cinnamon, cloves, and nutmeg
1 stick butter
12 eggs

Beat egg yolks. Add powdered sugar slowly and beat well. Then add nuts and crumbled zwieback and mix well. Next add spices and beat thoroughly. Fold in beaten egg whites.

Spread batter in pan and add butter. Bake 25-30 minutes in oven 375°F. While still warm, pour syrup over cake, and let soak in. (See recipe for syrup below.) Cut cake in small squares and serve.

SYRUP

1-1/2 cups honey
1 cup sugar
1-1/2 cups water

Boil sugar and water for thin syrup about 2 to 4 minutes. Then add honey. Cool, then pour slowly over cake. If a less sweet syrup is desired, use less honey and more water.

BIZCOCHITOS

These popular Southwestern cookies are rich, crisp, spicy and easy to make. Bizcochitos are served at coffees, teas and during the winter holidays.

6 cups sifted flour
3 teaspoons baking powder
1 teaspoon salt
1 pound lard or shortening (lard is traditional)
1-3/4 cups sugar
2 teaspoons anise seeds
2 eggs
1/4 cup brandy, or more
1 tablespoon ground cinnamon

Preheat oven to 350°F. Sift flour with baking powder and salt. Mix lard or shortening with 1-1/2 cups sugar and anise seeds with an electric mixer at medium speed.

Whip eggs until fluffy, and add to the creamed mixture. Add flour mixture and brandy and mix well until thoroughly blended. Use only enough brandy to form a stiff dough. Knead dough lightly and pat or roll to 1/4 to 1/2 inch thickness. Cut into fancy shapes. The fleur-de-lis shape is traditional for these cookies.

Sprinkle tops of cookies with a mixture of 1/4 cup sugar and cinnamon. Bake for 10 minutes, or until very lightly browned. Makes about 5 dozen.

BUNUELOS

4 eggs
1-1/4 cups sugar
2 cups all-purpose flour
1 teaspoon each baking powder and salt
vegetable oil
1 teaspoon ground cinnamon

In a large bowl, beat eggs and 1/4 cup of the sugar with an electric mixer until thick and lemon-colored. Blend together 1-1/2 cups of the flour, baking powder, and salt, then gradually add to egg mixture, beating until well mixed.

Stir in 1/4 cup more flour. Turn dough out onto a lightly floured board and knead gently, working in as little flour as necessary, until dough is smooth and no longer sticky (about 5 minutes). Divide dough into 16 equal pieces. With floured hands, shape each piece into a ball. Cover balls with plastic wrap as they are formed and let stand for 20 to 25 minutes. On a floured board, roll each ball into a 5-inch circle; stack circles, separating them with wax paper. In a wide, deep frying pan, heat 1-1/2 inches of oil to 350°F. on a deep-frying thermometer.

Meanwhile, combine remaining 1 cup sugar and 1 teaspoon cinnamon and sprinkle into a 9-inch round cake pan. Using tongs, push 1 circle of dough into hot oil and cook, turning once, until golden brown (about 1 1/2 minutes). Remove from oil, drain briefly, place in sugar mixture, and turn to coat thoroughly. Repeat until all Bunuelos are cooked; reserve any leftover sugar mixture. Serve bunuelos warm, sprinkling with reserved sugar mixture, if you like. Or let cool completely and store airtight at room temperature for up to 3 days (freeze for longer storage; thaw unwrapped).

To recrisp, arrange cooled or thawed bunuelos in double layers in shallow baking pans. Bake, uncovered, in a 350°F. oven until hot (6 to 8 minutes); sprinkle with reserved sugar mixture. Serve warm or cooled. Makes 16 Bunuelos.

PIÑON COOKIES

2 cups whole wheat flour
4 cups white flour
2 teaspoons baking powder
1 teaspoon salt
2 cups butter
1-1/2 cups sugar
1-3/4 cup water
1 cup shelled and chopped pinion nuts
cinnamon
sugar

Combine flour, baking powder, and salt. In another bowl, cream butter, and sugar until fluffy. Gradually add flour alternately with water until a stiff dough is formed. Add piñon nuts, blending thoroughly.

Roll out the dough on a lightly floured board to a 1/2-inch thickness. Cut into cookies with cookie cutters. Sprinkle cookies in equal amounts of cinnamon and sugar.

Bake cookies on a well-greased cookie sheet in a pre-heated 350°F. oven for about 15 minutes or until golden. Makes about 8 dozen.

NEW MEXICAN PRALINES

Pralines make a wonderful dessert following Mexican food. They are great for buffets when individually wrapped in colorful tissue paper and tied with ribbon. For holidays and parties, they are used for tree decorations or to liven up centerpieces.

1 cup firmly packed brown sugar
2 cups granulated sugar
3 tablespoons light corn syrup
1/4 teaspoon salt
1 cup light cream
4 tablespoons butter
2 teaspoons maple flavoring
1-1/2 cups shelled pecan halves

Butter a heavy 3-quart saucepan on the inside. Combine sugars, syrup, salt, cream and butter in the saucepan and stir until well blended. Cook slowly over medium heat until candy reaches the medium firm-ball stage (246°F.). Remove from heat. Let candy stand undisturbed for a few minutes. Then add flavoring and pecans and beat a few whips until creamy.

Drop by spoonfuls onto wax paper. If candy begins to harden, add a few drops of light cream; place over the lowest heat of the range and stir until creamy; it should drop smoothly from the spoon.

VARIATION: Milk or evaporated milk may be used instead of cream. If milk is substituted, use about 1 tablespoon more butter.

FLAMING MEXICAN BANANAS

*Enjoyed for centuries in Spain, this dessert was intro-
duced to the Southwest via Mexico with a touch of New
Orleans on the way.*

1/2 pound sweet butter
12 firm ripe bananas
1 cup light brown sugar
1 long continuous strip of orange peel
1/2 teaspoon ground cinnamon
Several gratings of fresh nutmeg (about 1/4 teaspoon)
1/2 cup light rum
1/2 cup white sugar
1/4 cup dark rum (151 proof)
12 scoops of very rich vanilla ice cream (about 2 pints)

Melt the butter in a large chafing dish, electric skillet,
or large cast iron skillet that can set on the grill. Place
the bananas in the butter, taking great care to not break
them. Sprinkle on the brown sugar. Add the orange
peel, cinnamon, and nutmeg.

Cook over low heat, gently rolling the bananas as they
cook to caramelize them slightly. Add the light rum after
about 5 minutes cooking time. When the bananas have
become light golden and glazed, sprinkle with the white
sugar and pour on the 151 rum. Ignite, keeping a lid or
some foil handy to dampen the flame if it gets out of control.

To serve, place the scoops of ice cream in large shallow
dessert dishes and place a banana alongside each, topping it with sauce. Serves 12.

LIME ICE

This dessert is so refreshing you'll want to prepare it for a real treat. You can make this a few days in advance, freeze, then let mellow 2 to 3 hours in the refrigerator before serving. You'll need an ice cream maker to prepare this dessert.

4-3/4 cups water
2-1/4 cups sugar
3 cups freshly squeezed lime juice
1/2 cup freshly squeezed lemon juice
1 tablespoon grated lime rind

Combine the water and sugar in a 2-quart saucepan. Simmer for 5 minutes to create a simple syrup. Remove from the heat and chill.

Pour the chilled mixture into the canister of your ice cream freezer. Add lime juice, lemon juice, and the lime rind. Mix with a wooden spoon or spatula. Follow the directions for your ice cream maker to create a firm ice.

To serve, form into balls with an ice cream scoop, dipping it into warm water between scoops. Serve in fluted sherbets but wineglasses-especially the tulip type—will also work. Makes 2-1/2 quarts.

TAMALE MASA

7 cups warm water
12 cups masa harina
3 cups shortening or lard
1-1/2 tablespoons salt
10 to 12 dozen dried corn husks cleaned and trimmed

Begin by soaking the corn husks in hot water (about 30 minutes). Add 7 cups warm water to the masa and stir to combine well, then allow to set for 15 or more minutes. The mixture should be the texture of a firm pudding—if too soft, add more masa; if hard and dry, add more warm water.

With an electric mixer on high, whip the shortening until very fluffy. Sprinkle in the salt, then add the masa a little at a time with the mixer running on low speed. When all has been well mixed, you are ready to roll tamales.

Using a rubber scraper, place 2 or more tablespoons of the masa mixture in a 3 X 4-inch rectangle of corn husk, centered lengthwise on each. The masa should be about 1/4 inch thick. Allow at least a 1-1/2 inch margin on the top and bottom. Place a thin strip of your choice of tamale filling down the very center. Hold the sides of the husks up, join them together, and roll to enclose the filling. Fold up the bottom, broader end, and tie using a strip of corn husk, fastening it with a bow. Then either crimp the tops together or fold down and tie with a strip of corn husk.

When you're ready to cook, place the tamales upright in a steaming basket, and steam tightly covered, for about 45 minutes, or until the masa is firm. Check while steaming to be sure there is at least an inch of water at all times to generate adequate steam.

PECAN-RAISIN DESSERT TAMALES

These sweet-tasting tamales are wonderful served after the hearty hot ones. In Mexico, where they are a much more frequent treat, tamales are considered more of a snack, either in midafternoon or late at night with hot Mexican Chocolate. Make these tamales for the holidays or for any time you want to celebrate with a festive meal. In addition to being steamed, they can also be toasted within the husk on a hot cast iron griddle. Just toast and turn until the husks are very browned. Toasted tamales will be gooey and spongy on the inside, instead of more solid as they are when steamed. Be sure to remove the husks before you eat.

1 recipe Tamale Masa (see recipe previous page)
2 cups sugar (can use half light brown sugar)
1-1/2 tablespoons cinnamon, or to taste
2-1/2 cups coarsely chopped pecans
3 cups raisins (use some light and dark for interest)
10 to 12 dozen corn husks

While the masa is still in the mixing bowl, add the sugar, cinnamon, and chopped pecans.

Spread masa mixture on soaked husks as described in the masa recipe on the previous page. Next sprinkle about 1-1/2 tablespoons raisins in a strip down the center.

Fold and tie with strips of husk. Steam as in Tamale Masa recipe on the previous page. Makes 10 to 12 dozen.

Variation: Almost any type of preserves can be substituted for the raisins. Candied fruit can also be used.

Santa Fe Bob Sez:

An old favorite dessert in New Mexico is Capirotada, a bread pudding, often called "sopa." Since New Mexico was cut off from the rest of Mexico by long distances, in the early days the missions were supplied by wagon trains which came once every two years from Mexico. They brought wines, fruit, tree seeds and grape shoots, chocolate, cheeses and delicacies from Europe for the French and Spanish priests. Many apple orchards of New Mexico probably grew from seeds brought by priests from Europe in the very early days. Capirotada was discovered by the mountain men and travelers to New Mexico in the early 1800's. They had trouble with Spanish pronunciation and preferred to call it "Spotted Dog" because of the raisins in the dish. A later variation of this dish was prepared by the chuck wagon cooks during the cattle period, and was called "Spotted Pup".

CAPIROTADA

2 cups toasted bread
4 eggs
2 cups milk
1 cup raisins in hot water
1/2 pound brown sugar
2 tablespoons cinnamon
1 teaspoon nutmeg
1/2 onion
1/2 pound. melted butter
1 cup Longhorn cheese
2 cups sliced apples

Break up toasted bread, preferably old, dry bread. In another bowl, beat eggs well and add milk. Separately, put raisins in 1 cup hot water to cover. Allow to soak and plump for five minutes, and drain. Add dark-brown sugar to the milk-egg mixture and mix in with sliced apples. Add cinnamon, and nutmeg. Chop onion fine. Mix all thoroughly with the bread and moisten with butter melted in 2 cups hot water.

Grate Longhorn cheese. Place layers of the pudding in a casserole, alternately with layers of the cheese. Bake at 350°F. about 45 minutes, and serve hot. Sprinkle with colorful candy sprinkles.

SPICED CARMEL CUSTARD FLAN

4 whole cloves
2 each whole allspice and cardamom pods, crushed
1 cinnamon stick (about 2 inches long), broken in half
2 cups milk
1 teaspoon vanilla
2/3 cup sugar
6 eggs

In a cheesecloth bag or a tea ball, combine cloves, all-spice, cardamom, and cinnamon stick. Place in a 2-quart pan with milk and vanilla; set aside.

In a small frying pan, melt 1/3 cup of the sugar over medium heat, shaking and tilting pan until sugar is caramelized. Immediately pour syrup into a 9-inch pie pan at least 1-1/2 inches deep. Using hot pads, tilt pan quickly so syrup flows over bottom and slightly up sides. If syrup hardens before you finish, set pan over medium heat to soften.

Heat milk and spices over medium heat until steaming hot, then remove from heat and let cool slightly; remove spices. This process intensifies the spicy flavor and shortens the baking time. In a large bowl, beat eggs with remaining 1/3 cup sugar; gradually add heated milk, stirring quickly with a fork.

Set caramel-lined pan in a larger pan and pour in egg mixture. Add enough boiling water to larger pan so it just comes up around edges of pie pan. Bake in a 350° oven until a 3/8-inch-deep crevice forms when you gently push center of custard with back of a spoon (about 15 minutes). Remove flan from hot water and refrigerate immediately for at least 6 hours or until next day.

To serve, loosen edge of flan with a knife, then cover pan with a rimmed plate. Holding both together, quickly invert. To serve, cut into wedges and spoon caramel sauce on top. Makes 6 to 8 servings.

SOUR MILK COFFEE CAKE

2 tablespoons butter
1 cup sugar
1 egg, beaten
1 teaspoons soda
1 cup sour milk
2 cups flour
2 teaspoons baking powder
1/2 teaspoon salt
1/2 teaspoon cinnamon
1/4 teaspoon nutmeg
2 tablespoons butter, melted

In a large bowl, cream butter and sugar until light and fluffy. Blend in beaten egg. Dissolve soda in the cup of sour milk and set aside.

Sift all dry ingredients together in separate bowl. Then add dry ingredients and sour milk alternately to egg/butter mixture. Pour batter into a greased, shallow pan and sprinkle melted butter over top. Then mix the topping as follows.

TOPPING

3 tablespoons brown sugar
1 tablespoon flour
1 tablespoons cinnamon

Mix all ingredients in a bowl with a pastry blender. Sprinkle over top. Bake in 350° F. oven for 25 minutes.

COUNTRY STYLE CHOCOLATE CAKE

Made with mashed potatoes!

2/3 cup butter
2 cups sugar
4 egg yolks, beaten
1 cup hot mashed potatoes
1 teaspoon vanilla
1/2 cup cocoa (unsweetened)
2 cups cake flour
1/2 teaspoon salt
2 teaspoons baking powder
1/2 teaspoon. cinnamon
1 teaspoon cloves
1/2 teaspoon nutmeg
1 cup milk
1 cup chopped nuts
4 egg whites

In a large bowl, cream butter and sugar until fluffy. Beat in egg yolks. Blend in mashed potatoes, vanilla, then cocoa.

In separate bowl, sift together remaining dry ingredients and alternately add them to sugar/potato mixture along with the milk.

Beat egg whites to stiff-peak stage. Fold in nuts, then egg whites. Pour the batter into two buttered loaf pans (5 x 9inch) or a 13 x 9 x 2 inch pan. Bake in 350° F. oven for 40-50 minutes.

CUSTARD PIE

A custard is a cooked, sweetened mixture of milk and eggs. Custards were very popular in the Old West before instant pudding, flavored gelatin, and store-bought ice cream became available. Plain ones were prescribed for children and invalids, while dessert custards were made in such flavors as coconut, apple, pumpkin, caramel, persimmon, and rhubarb.

Lemon rind and nutmeg were the usual flavorings for custard pies. Modern cooks would use vanilla. With a topping of meringue or whipped cream this becomes a cream pie.

2 cups whole milk
lemon rind
nutmeg, a few gratings
3 eggs
1/3 cup of granulated sugar
a pinch of salt
1 tablespoon of flour

Prepare nine-inch pie crust and line buttered pie pan. Prick the crust all over with a fork to prevent bubbling, and bake it in a preheated oven at 425°F for 10 minutes. If the crust rises up despite pricking, press it down with another pie pan before it cools.

In the saucepan heat the milk just to boiling. Score and shave the lemon rind into the milk; add nutmeg.

In the bowl beat the eggs; then beat in the sugar, salt, and flour. Gradually stir in the hot milk and lemon rind mixture. Pour the custard into the saucepan and stir it over medium heat until it coats the stirring spoon with a creamy film.

Pour the custard into the pie shell and bake in the oven at 425° for 10 minutes. Reduce heat to 350° and continue to bake until the filling is browned and a knife inserted comes out clean. This will take an additional 25 to 30 minutes. Serve at room temperature.

PUEBLO PEACH CRISP

6 fresh peaches, pitted and cut into
3/4-inch slices (5-6 cups)
1/4 cup white sugar
1/4 teaspoon salt
3/4 cup flour
3/4 cup brown sugar
1/2 cup butter

Place peaches in a shallow baking pan or casserole. Mix white sugar and salt and sprinkle over peaches. Combine flour and brown sugar in a mixing bowl and cut in butter until mixture is formed into small balls. Sprinkle mixture over peaches.

Bake in a preheated 375°F. oven for about 45 minutes or until top is lightly brown and crumbly. Serve warm and top with whipped cream or scoop of vanilla ice cream. Serves 6 to 8.

Beverages and Spirits

Although there were many kinds of drinks enjoyed by the inhabitants of the Old West, some of the most noteworthy were those beverages and spirits enjoyed in saloons. In the early days, the saloon existed because it filled many basic human needs. It was a place of comfort, a refuge, even a place of refinement where one could rub elbows with a fellow human being. It was a place where cowboys could talk about the round-up, and where settlers could tell tales about farming, livestock, and the hardships they endured. The saloon was a place to dispel the loneliness of a month on the range or two months in the back country.

And then there were those who spent most of the day and a good part of their nights in saloons. Besides being a drinking place, a saloon was a diner, a hotel, a bath and comfort station, a livery stable, gambling hall, dance club, bordello, barbershop, courtroom, church, social club, political hub, dueling ground, post office, sports arena, undertaker's parlor, library, news stand, theater, opera, city hall, employment agency, museum, trading post, grocery store, ice cream parlor, even a forerunner of the movie house where fascinated cowboys cranked the handles of ornate kinetoscopes to watch the jerky movements of exotic cancan dancers. A saloon could fulfill some or all of these functions.

Someone once said that, with the exception of the Battle of the Little Bighorn, all western history was made inside the saloons. There is a grain of truth in this. States were named, capitals founded, candidates announced, and elections held inside barrooms. The saloon was as American as apple pie, in the best tradition of the Founding Fathers.

The first full-fledged western saloon was opened a generation before the existence of roads and the coming of the wagon trains. It was founded in 1822 by a trapper named Brown in a place appropriately called Brown's Hole. Located where the present states of Wyoming, Colorado, and Utah meet, this saloon catered to mountain men. It was here that a yearly "Great Rendezvous" was held where beaver men, trappers, and all sorts of mountain men congregated to barter their pelts for baubles and beads for their Indian squaws and for a year's supply of tobacco, hardtack, powder, lead, and liquor for themselves. They also came to meet old friends and to go on the wildest, most complete drunk imaginable.

The westerner was a drinking man. Every boy looked forward to that moment when his voice changed and he could strut up to the bar, slam his two bits down, and say, in as deep a voice as he could muster, "Gimme a whiskey." The urge to prop one's foot on a brass rail and lean an elbow on the bar was almost universal. Young males were expected to join in or they were considered effeminate. Getting drunk together was a special male privilege that bonded men together in a sort of brotherhood which might last their lifetime.

One seldom-mentioned but generally excluded minority was, of course, women. The saloon customer did not want them around unless they were pretty waitresses or ladies of the night. The old tale, however, that respectable women never, never entered the western saloon has to be taken with more than a grain of salt. In larger cities women sooner or later, generally sooner, asserted their right to a public drink and were sometimes provided with a discreet ladies' side entrance. Visitors to San Francisco in the pioneer era pretended to be shocked by women openly drinking at bars, gambling among men, and strolling tipsily in the streets. The same was true in early Denver, but emancipation of the drinking woman was a lengthy process. In the smaller towns of cattle country an unspoken taboo against women in saloons lasted until after World War I.

In the Old West, saloon patrons experienced that "loosening of the tongue" the same as they do today, except the subject matter was different. Cowboys would tell bawdy stories and sing ribald songs only when they were in camp. In the saloons they talked about horses and beef, and told how to handle them and bragged about how good they were at it. It was the same with team-hands, railroaders and loggers. Men did their best work in the saloons and their best drinking and women-chasing when they were out on the job.

In areas closer to the border with Mexico, gallons of beer, tequila, and rum mixtures were traditionally imbibed along with the traditional menu of spicy foods. Usually, a tequila drink was served before meals. Tequila, undoubtedly Mexico's most popular drink, has been widely adopted by Southwesterners. In addition to tequila in mixed drinks, true veterans enjoy it served simply by the shot with a half of lime and a saucer of coarse salt. To indulge, the lime is placed between the thumb and forefinger and a pinch of salt is placed on the thumb knuckle. Before each sip, a lick of salt is taken, then a suck of lime.

The most well-known tequila drink is the Margarita, a lime-based drink, served in frosty, salt-rimmed glasses.

As fruits became more widely cultivated, drinks that included peaches, bananas or strawberries soon became popular.

Dry wines were served alongside a meal, as well as Sangria. Ale, beer, and wine were common as family drinks where milk was in short supply. Many found, in the cold of a covered wagon or cabin, that "an ounce of firewater in the belly is worth a pound of wool on the back." The firewater might be whiskey or a highly alcoholic medicine.

For adults, coffee (sweetened with molasses) was the favorite everyday drink. Over a century ago world coffee prices skyrocketed when disaster struck Ceylon, the principal producer. The British promptly substituted tea, but Americans, still remembering the Boston Tea Party, remained devoted to coffee. Poor as they were, no one would have departed on the trail West without their grinder and a supply of coffee beans.

HUNTER'S COFFEE

This coffee is particularly good on cold mornings to send a hunter off into the woods or a ranch hand off to work.

1 cup ground coffee
1 tall can milk
2/3 quart water
2 tablespoons butter
sugar

Put the coffee in a pot and bring to boiling. Punch a hole in a can of sweet milk and set it in a pan of simmering water about an inch deep. After the coffee has steeped until it has become very strong, and bubbles rise from the hole in the can of milk, pour the coffee in another pot, leaving the grounds behind. Add the milk, and stir in the butter. Even people who do not ordinarily take sugar in their coffee will want some sugar in this strong coffee.

COFFEE BOSTON

This coffee, made in western saloons, was called Coffee Boston and was a favorite with gamblers and others who had extended themselves the night before.

medium cream
butter
sugar

Heat a heavy porcelain cup on the stove until too hot to pick up. Wrap a cloth around the cup, set on the counter and fill it almost halfway with cream. When the handle has cooled, fill the cup with hot, strong coffee. Add a small lump of butter, and serve with sugar.

MEXICAN COFFEE

water
dark roast coffee
1 teaspoon ground cinnamon for each of 8 cups

Add cinnamon to the top of the coffee grounds, then brew coffee as usual. Serve in earthenware or pottery mugs.

Variation: Many like to serve dark brown sugar or piloncillo with the coffee. Or you can add about 1/2 cup to the pot before serving. Piloncillo is unrefined sugar, golden in color and with a more caramel flavor than granulated white sugar. You can find it in the Mexican foods section of your local grocery store or at a specialty shop.

HAYMAKER'S SWITCHEL

3/4 gallon of fresh cold water
1/2 cup light molasses
1 cup brown sugar
2 cups apple cider vinegar

Mix ingredients together and serve over ice. You might wish to add more molasses and taste it as you make it, for some vinegars are much stronger than others. It should be a pleasant sweet and sour spicy drink.

HOT WASSAIL

Squeeze and reserve the juice of 2 oranges and 2 lemons. In a tightly covered saucepan simmer together for one hour: the squeezed orange and lemon halves, 2 sticks of cinnamon, 2 teaspoons whole or ground cloves, 1 cup sugar, and 1 1/2 quarts water. Strain mixture and add 1 gallon fresh apple cider. Mix all together, reheat and serve hot with crackers and cheese. This is a very good drink for cold weather.

MEXICAN CHOCOLATE

2 squares sweet chocolate
1 quart milk or cream
1 egg
1/2 teaspoon vanilla
pinch nutmeg
1/4 teaspoon cinnamon
pinch ground, dry orange peel

Simply add hot milk or cream to sweet chocolate, add egg, vanilla, and cinnamon. Blend for 2 minutes. Start blender at slow speed, or the hot milk will splash. You may add just a pinch of ground orange peel. Blend until frothy. Top cups with a sprinkle of nutmeg.

PINOLE

This basic Mexican Indian drink is healthful, nourishing and delicious.

1 cup masa harina, or ordinary corn meal, ground fine
1/2 teaspoon powdered cinnamon
3 cups milk
1/4 cup sugar

Roast corn meal in a 450°F. oven for 4-6 minutes until golden brown, but not burned. Spread the meal evenly over a cookie sheet, and move it around twice while roasting by using a spoon. Cool, then add 1 part sugar to 4 parts corn meal, and flavor with powdered cinnamon. Add 1/2 cup cold water to moisten, then cook slowly in hot milk for about 15 minutes. Be careful not to let the meal burn on the bottom of your pot. Stir constantly. Use as much pinole mix to milk as you would hot chocolate mix to water in making a medium strong cup. When the corn meal is soft, pour into cups and drink. It's consistency should be the same as a medium thick cup of hot chocolate.

CHERRY BOUNCE

5 pints dark cherries
1 pound brown sugar
1 quart dark rum or cognac

Grind cherries through a meat grinder, seeds and all. Place them in a bottle of dark rum or cognac. Let them steep for one week. Strain the mixture through cheese cloth, and add brown sugar. Place in a glass container and seal. Allow to age for two weeks before enjoying.

Santa Fe Bob Sez:

Be real careful with these concoctions! They can be sneakier than a snake and bite just as mean.

Liquor was strictly forbidden on the roundup, but now and again a bottle was smuggled in. There is a story told about one humerous incident that occurred involving a particulary ornery Southerner who was the camp cook. One afternoon a cowboy heard shooting in the vicinity of the chuckwagon and came riding in to see what was happening.

The cook was stirring beans in a pot with the barrel of his Colt pistol. He was then casually expelling those beans that adhered to the inside of the barrel by shooting at a nearby rock. When the cowpuncher asked about his unusual cooking method, the cook replied that he was tesing the beans to find out when they were soft enough to eat.!

Of course camp cooks were universally well-known for their grouchiness and that reputation was evidenced by the old saying that "Only a fool argues with a skunk, a mule or a cook."

INJUN WHISKEY

The Indians became used to this type of whiskey, and in the 1860's, when good whiskey finally came west, the Indians rejected it because it just didn't have the "good old flavor". Unscrupulous traders would doctor their "Injun Whiskey" with laudanum (tincture of opium) in order to prevent violence among the Indians after heavy drinking. Some did over-dose and die.

During trading at Indian camps, the chief got to sample the contents of whiskey barrels to assure fellow tribesmen that it was worth the furs being traded. After the trades were concluded, the traders left camp before the whiskey was distributed, as they wished to avoid the violent party which inevitably followed.

1 quart corn whiskey or Bourbon
3 or 4 hot red peppers
cut plug tobacco or tobacco from 2 cigarettes
a thumb pinch of old-fashioned black gun powder,
not modern nitrated gunpowder
1 cup water divided between two small cooking pots

Boil peppers for 10 minutes to make a tea in one pot of water. Do the same with the tobacco in a second pot. Strain and cook down by half. Add both to the whiskey and put a pinch of gunpowder into the bottle. The pinch of black gunpowder gives a special smooth taste. **Be sure to use the old-fashioned black powder made of saltpeter, sulphur, and charcoal, because modern nitrated high speed powders are poisonous.**

―――――――――――――――――――――――――――――――

BRIGHT RED
CHOKECHERRY WINE

4 gallons red chokecherries
water as needed
brandy or grain alcohol
1 cup pounded chokecherry pits
8 pounds sugar
yeast cake

Pick the chokecherries early when they are red, just turning ripe. Heat in warm water to soften. Crush and place in a crock with a gallon of warm water. Add 1 pound of sugar and a yeast cake. Decant the juice after a day and put the juice in a 5-gallon keg. Add 1 pound of sugar to the keg, mix, cork lightly, and cover with a clean, damp burlap bag. After another day, add 1 gallon of water to the berries, 1 pound of sugar, and let work another day.

Press out the juice, discard the berries. Add the juice to that already in the keg, stir in the remainder of the 8 pounds of sugar, fill with water to the 4-1/2 gallon point, cork lightly, cover as before, and allow to work for several days.

Keep close watch and when the fermentation starts to subside but the wine is still sweet, add brandy or alcohol in sufficient quantity to kill the fermentation. Cork tightly and leave for about 6 weeks. In that time the wine should be a clear scarlet and have the marked flavor of maraschino cherries. Recask, filling the keg to the cork with a 20 percent mixture of alcohol and water, perhaps in the form of brandy or vodka mixed with water one-for-one. A cupful of cracked chokecherry stones will increase the cherry flavor.

JALAPEÑO MARTINIS

For this recipe, simply prepare your favorite martini, substituting a round of pickled jalapeño for a lemon twist, olive or pickled onion.

If you don't usually make martinis, just get a shaker or a nice glass or silver pitcher and a long-handled spoon. For 6 good-sized drinks, put several ice cubes in the shaker or pitcher and add half a bottle of premium gin or vodka (measures 24 ounces, or 3 liquid measuring cups) and a generous optional splash of dry vermouth. Some omit the vermouth and add a splash of juice from the pickled jalapeños. Be careful if you are inexperienced with this! You may want to sample the proportions ahead of time. Mix vigorously or shake until well mixed. Serve garnished with a round of pickled jalapeño. For an added touch, place the martini glasses in the freezer about one half hour before serving the drinks.

TOM AND JERRY

Use one large and one small china bowl. Beat the whites of 12 fresh eggs to a stiff froth in the large bowl, adding 1 heaping tablespoon of sugar for each egg. Beat yolks of eggs separately in the small bowl, adding a pinch of baking soda. Beat to a stiff batter. Then mix the two batters together, stir frequently so as to prevent the sugar sticking to the bottom.

To serve Tom and Jerry:

Put 2 tablespoons of the above mixture into a large mug. Add 1 drink (2 ounces) liquor and fill with boiling water. Stir well while adding the water. Spoon a dollop of egg mixture on top and sprinkle with cinnamon or nutmeg.

MARGARITA

These are the most traditional Mexican cocktails. The touch of froth added by the egg white is a recent twist.

salt
1/2 ounce Triple Sec
1-1/2 ounces tequila
ice

After lime juice is extracted, rub the lime rind around the edge of a chilled martini or wine glass. Invert rim of glass onto a generously salted surface and lightly twist the edge of the glass into salt to form a salty crust on the rim. If time permits, freeze the glasses for a frosty appearance. Shake all ingredients together with ice or blend together in a blender. Taste and add more lime or Triple Sec if desired. Pour into the salt-rimmed glass.

Variation: For an extra frothy Margarita, add about one-quarter of an egg white to the mixture before blending, and whip until frothy.

DANDELION WINE

1 quart dandelion blossoms, loosely packed
1 gallon hot soft water
juice and rind of l lemon
2 oranges
2 pounds of sugar
1 cake of yeast

Pour water over blossoms, let stand overnight. Drain. Add lemon,oranges and sugar. Stir in sugar well, add 1 cake yeast. Let stand one week in a warm room. Strain and bottle, putting corks in loosely.

MEXICAN GRASSHOPPER

1 ounce Kahlua
1 ounce green creme de menthe
1 ounce heavy cream crushed ice

Pour the ingredients into a blender, add crushed ice and blend thoroughly until frothy. Serve in a chilled glass.

TEQUILA SUNRISE PUNCH

8 cups orange juice
1-1/2 to 2 cups tequila
1/2 cup grenadine syrup
ice cubes
orange slices

In a chilled 3 to 4-quart pitcher or small punch bowl mix the orange juice, tequila, and grenadine. Add ice and orange slices.

COWPUNCHER'S EYEOPENER

1-1/2 ounces of cognac
1 tablespoon vinegar
1 teaspoon catsup
1 tablespoon Worcestershire
1 teaspoon Angostura
1 small glass vegetable juice

Mix in dark colored glass chilled with chipped ice. Drop in yolk of raw egg, and pinch of black pepper. Tip glass, being careful not to break egg yolk.

MARGARITA WINE PUNCH

In a punch bowl, stir together 3 cans (6 oz. each)
thawed frozen limeade concentrate, 1 can (12 oz.)
thawed frozen lemonade concentrate, and 1 bottle (1.5
liters) plus 1 bottle (750 ml.) cold dry white wine.
Shortly before serving, add ice cubes. Makes 3 quarts.

SANGRIA PUNCH WITH FRUIT

Up to a day ahead, stir together 1/4 cup each sugar
and orange-flavored liqueur. Add 1 medium-size orange,
thinly sliced and seeded. Cover and refrigerate; stir
occasionally. In a punch bowl, combine sugar mixture
with 1 bottle (1.5 liters) cold rosé wine, 1 bottle (750 ml.)
cold burgundy wine, 1 cup orange juice, and 1/4 cup
sugar. Before serving, add 1 unpeeled red-skinned apple
(thinly sliced) and ice cubes. Makes 3 quarts.

TOMATO-ORANGE SANGRITA

In a large pitcher, combine 1 cup tomato juice, 2 cups
orange juice, 1/2 cup lemon or lime juice, and 1/4 teaspoon liquid hot pepper seasoning. Pour into ice-filled
tumblers. Add green onions (with tops) for stirrers.
Makes 4 servings.

EGGNOG

Eggnog has a long tradition of use on festive occasions. Recipes have always called for rum or brandy or both. Even the abstemious Shakers used apple brandy in eggnog prepared for the sick. Eggnog drunk in the hay-fields sometimes contained hard cider.

6 eggs, separated
1/2 cup granulated sugar
1 quart mil,
2 cups heavy cream
1/2 teaspoon ground nutmeg or cinnamon
9 ounces rum or brandy

Beat the egg yolks and sugar in the bowl until blended. Slowly beat in the milk, then thoroughly stir in the cream. Refrigerate this mixture while you beat the egg whites until they form soft peaks. Pour chilled mixture into a punch bowl and add rum or brandy. Top with the beaten egg whites, and stir deeply a few times. Sprinkle the nutmeg or cinnamon over the foamy surface and carefully ladle into cups so as not to disturb the foam. Makes six servings.

ROSE WINE

A lovely wine can be made of the rosebuds that form on wild roses after the roses fall off. Make the same as choke cherry wine (see previous recipe), except run the buds through a good chopper. When you put the sugar in the juice, add one yeast cake.

TOMBSTONE HOME BREW

1 five gallon crock
1 three foot syphon hose
1 bottle capper
1 box bottle caps
50 beer bottles
2 1/2 pounds sugar
1 cup rice,
1 teaspoon salt
1 can red top malt.

To 1 gallon water heated to boiling add sugar, rice, salt and malt. Heat, stirring all the time, until it just comes to a boil. Pour into 4 gallons of cold water already placed in the crock. Stir and add 1 package of dry yeast, (or fresh dissolved in luke warm water). Cover with cloth. Skim as needed and bottle when it has finished working but is just sparkling (3 to 5 days).

Never let the first high foam turn over into the beer. Skim off the foam and syphon the brew carefully to avoid stirring the sediment. If it is bottled while still working it will burst the bottles and if there are too many sparkles it will be all foam when bottles are opened. (Four or five sparkles a minute is about right). If it goes flat, bottle and put 1/4 teaspoon sugar in each bottle before you cap it. Let stand 3 to 6 days. The longer the better.

GINGER WATER

Modern ginger ale has two ancestors. One is ginger beer, which was brewed and bottled at home like root beer. A fermented, bubbly drink, it was sometimes alcoholic, mostly not. The other is ginger water, or "switchel," as New Englanders called it, a nonalcoholic drink prepared for farmers during long hot days of working in the fields. Modern commercial refreshers for athletes have the same thirst-quenching tartness.

Ginger comes from the root of a tropical plant. In the Old West, cooks in port cities bought and used fresh ginger root in their cooking, but what reached the pioneers was usually already dried and ground to a powder.

1/2 to 3/4 cup, packed brown sugar
1 teaspoon powdered ginger
1/2 cup cider vinegar
2-quart jug with funnel
other half-gallon container

Dissolve brown sugar and ginger in vinegar by shaking or stirring. Add 1 quart of cold water, mix, and serve. Makes six servings.

SCOTCH BEER

1 peck malt
4 ounces hops
1 ounce coriander seeds
1 pound honey
2 ounces orange peel
1 ounce bruised ginger

Add 1 peck malt to 4 gallons of boiling water and let it mash for 8 hours. Then strain and in the strained liquor boil hops, coriander, honey, orange peel, and bruised ginger. Boil for half an hour, then strain again. Begin fermentation by stirring in one package of dry yeast. Cover with a cloth. Skim as necessary and bottle when it has finished fermenting in about 3 to 5 days.

Home Remedies
& Household Hints

HOME REMEDIES

One hundred years ago people in the Old West lived so far away from civilization and doctors that in case of illness they had to use the things nature provided. Many remedies from old-timers, cowpunchers, and roundup cooks are based in folk medicine that still has some validity today. **However, these remedies are NOT RECOMMENDED FOR USE***...they are merely listed here for you to get an idea of how people in the Old West lived.*

For chills: Pick the leaves of the wild native sage, wash, put a cup full on back of stove, pour boiling water (about 3 cups) over the leaves and let steep 30 minutes. Drink hot, stay in bed, and keep warm with hot water bottles.

For boils: To draw or bring a boil to a head, gather some native cactus, burn off the spines, then wash cactus in warm water. Lay cactus on a board and mash to a pulp, put the cactus pulp on a piece of cheese cloth. Warm this poultice in the oven, then place on the boil. This was used for animals, too. ALSO, the skin of a boiled egg is recommended remedy that can be applied to a boil. Peel it carefully, wet and apply to the part affected. It will draw out the matter, and relieve the soreness in a few hours.

For gall bladder colic: Drink 15 drops of fluid extract of dandelion in a little warm water.

For hoarseness: Mix 1 teaspoon of glycerine with the well-beaten egg white. Add juice of 1 lemon and enough water to make palatable.

For hiccups: 5 drops camphor dropped in 1 teaspoon sugar.

For sore throat and hoarseness: A towel wrung out of cold water and wrapped around throat with dry towel. This helps you to sleep when ill with sore throat.

To drop medicine without a dropper: Shake the bottle to moisten the cork. With the wet end of the cork moisten the edges of the mouth of the bottle, then holding the cork under the mouth, let the fluid pass over the cork in dripping.

To prevent bedsores: Apply to the tender parts of the body with a feather, a mixture made by beating to a strong froth, the white of an egg, and dropping in while beating, 2 teaspoons of wine. Bottle for use.

Cure for leanness: Leanness is generally caused by lack of power in the digestive organs to digest and assimilate the fat producing food. First restore digestion, take plenty of sleep, drink all the water the stomach will bear in the morning on rising, take moderate exercise in the open air. Eat oatmeal, cracked wheat, Graham mush, baked sweet apples, roasted and boiled beef. Cultivate jolly people, and bathe daily.

For toothache: The worst toothache, or neuralgia coming from the teeth, may be speedily and delightfully ended by the application of a bit of clean cotton, saturated in a solution of ammonia, to the defective tooth. Sometimes the sufferer is prompted to momentary laughter by the application, but the pain will disappear.

Another method for the toothache: One teaspoon of powdered alum, and an equal amount of fine salt well mixed, applied to the gums by dipping your moistened finger in the mixed powder. Also put some on the tooth, and keep rubbing the gums with it.

To cure earache: Take a bit of cotton batting, put in a pinch of black pepper, gather it up and tie it, dip it in sweet oil, and insert it in the ear. Put a flannel bandage over the head to keep it warm; it often gives immediate relief.
Another remedy: Take equal parts of tincture of opium and glycerine. Mix in a warm teaspoon and drop 2 or 3 drops into the ear. Stop the ear with cotton. Repeat every hour if needed.

To stop the flow of blood: For a slight cut there is nothing better to control the hemorrhage than common unglazed brown wrapping paper, such as used in markets and grocers; a piece to be bound over the wound. Also a handful of flour bound on the cut, or cobwebs and brown sugar, pressed on like lint.

When an artery is cut the blood spurts out at each pulsation. Press the thumb firmly over the artery near the wound, and on the side towards the heart. Press hard enough to stop bleeding, and wait for the physician to come. The wounded person is often able to do this himself, if he knows what to do.

For diarrhea: Brown to scorching, two tablespoonfuls of flour in a cast iron skillet. Add enough water to make it drinkable. Give a teaspoonful of this solution every 30 minutes until diarrhea stops. This has been known to be very successful.

Relief from Asthma: Sufferers from asthma should get a muskrat skin and wear it over their lungs with the fur side next to the body. It will bring certain relief.

Grandmother's cough syrup: Take half pound of dry hoarhound herbs, 1 pod of red pepper, 4 tablespoonfuls of ginger, boil in all 3 quarts of water, then strain. Add 1 teaspoonful of good, fresh tar, and a pound of sugar. Boil slowly and stir often, until it is reduced to 1 quart of syrup. When cool, bottle for use. Take 1 or 2 teaspoonful 4 or 6 times a day.

For Rheumatism: Take 2 eggs, 1 gill of vinegar, 1 gill of New England Rum, 1 teaspoonful of spirits of turpentine, 1 teaspoonful of sunfish oil. Beat the eggs up well first, then add a small quantity of each article at a time, until all are mixed, stirring the mixture all the time. Bathe the affected parts with it 2 or 3 times a day.

For a Caked Breast: Bake large potatoes, put 2 or more in a woolen stocking; crush them soft and apply to the breast as hot as can be borne; repeat constantly till relieved.

Stop a bloody nose: Roll up a piece of paper and press it under the upper lip. In obstinate cases, blow a little gum arabic up the nostril through a quill, which will immediately stop the discharge. Powdered alum, dissolved in water, is also good. Pressure by the finger over the small artery near the ala (Wing) of the nose, on the side where the blood is flowing, is said to arrest the hemorrhage immediately. Sometimes by wringing a cloth out of very hot water, and laying it across the back of the neck, gives relief. Napkins wrung out of cold water must be laid across the forehead and nose, the hands dipped in cold water, and a bottle of hot water applied to the feet.

To take cinders from the eye: Take a horse-hair and double it, leaving a loop. If the object can be seen, lay the loop over it, close the eye, and the mote will come out as the hair is withdrawn. If the irritating object cannot be seen, raise the lid of the eye high as possible and place the loop as far as you can, close the eye and roll the ball around a few times, draw out the hair, and the substance which caused the pain will be sure to come with it. This method is practiced by axemakers and other workers in steel.

For sunstroke: Wrap a wet cloth bandage over the head; wet another cloth, folded small, square, cover it thickly with salt, and bind it on the back of the neck; apply dry salt behind the ears. Put mustard plasters to the calves of the legs and soles of the feet. This is an effectual remedy.

To remove warts: Wash with water saturated with common washing-soda, and let it dry without wiping. Repeat frequently until they disappear. Or, pass a pin through the wart and hold one end of it over the flame of a candle or lamp until the wart fires by the heat, and it will disappear.

For severe sprains: The white of an egg, a tablespoonful of vinegar and a tablespoonful of spirits of turpentine. Mix in a bottle, shake thoroughly, and bathe the sprain as soon as possible after the accident. This should be remembered by everyone as it is of great value. Another invaluable remedy for a sprain is wormwood boiled in vinegar and applied hot, with enough cloths wrapped around it to keep the sprain moist.

The Sun's cholera mixture: Asiatic cholera was a dreaded disease many years ago. Learned doctors from both hemispheres drew up a prescription which was called "The Sun Cholera Mixture." It is to be found the best remedy for looseness of the bowels ever yet devised.

Take equal parts of tincture of cayenne, tincture of opium, tincture of rhubarb, essence of peppermint, and spirits of camphor. Mix well. Dose 15 drops to 30 drops in a wine-glass of water, according to age and violence of the attack. Repeat every 15 or 20 minutes until relief is obtained. Even when no cholera is anticipated, it is a valuable remedy for summer complaints, and should always be kept in readiness.

For Felons: Take common rock salt, as used for salting down pork or beef, dry in an oven, and pound it fine and mix with spirits of turpentine in equal parts; put it in rag and wrap it around the parts affected; as it gets dry put on more, and in 24 hours you are cured. The felon will be dead.

Tape Worms: Tape worms are said to be removed by refraining from supper and breakfast, and at eight o'clock taking 1/3 part of 200 minced pumpkin seeds, the shells of which have been removed by hot water; at nine take another 1/3, at ten the remainder, and follow it at eleven with a strong dose of castor oil.

Grandmother's family spring bitters: Mandrake root, 1 ounce; dandelion root, 1 ounce; burdock root, 1 ounce; yellow dock root, 1 ounce; prickly ash berries, 2 ounces; marshmallow, 1 ounce; turkey rhubarb, 1/2 ounce; gentian, 1 ounce; English camomileflowers, 1 ounce; red clover tops, 2 ounces.

Wash the herbs and roots; put them into an earthen vessel, pour over 2 quarts of water that has been boiled and cooled; let it stand overnight and soak; in the morning, set it on the back of the stove, and steep it 5 hours; it must not boil, but nearly ready to boil. Strain it through a cloth, and add half a pint of good gin. Keep it in a cool place. Half a wine-glass taken as a dose twice a day.

Infants cordial: Pleurisy-root, scull-cap, skunk-cabbage, hops, cramp-bark, prickly ashberries, calamus, angelica seed, sassafras, of each, one ounce; ginger, capsicure, of each 2 drachmas. Pour on 6 pints of boiling water; when cold, add 3 pints of good Holland Gin, and 2 pounds of loaf-sugar. Let it stand 2 weeks, frequently shaking.

Bailey's Itch Ointment: Olive-oil, 1 pound; suet, 1 pound; alkanet root, 2 ounces. Melt and macerate until colored; then strain, and add 3 ounces each of alum nitre, and sulphate of zinc, in very fine powder, adding vermillion to color it, and oil of aniseed, lavender, and thyme to perfume.

To make fever and ague pills: Quinine, 20 grains; Dovers-powders, 10 grain; sub-carbonate of iron, 10 grains. Mix with mucilage of gum arabic, and make into 20 pills. Dose: 2 pills every hour, beginning four or five hours before the chill is expected. When the chills have been broken, take 1 pill night and morning for a month, to prevent a return.

Santa Fe Bob Sez:

Sarsaparilla syrup was good for just about anything that ailed 'ya! Camp cooks used to make it with one pound of Sarsaparilla root, one pound of sugar and 5 quarts of boiling water. First, cut or chop up the Sarsaparilla root into short pieces, the shorter the better, put it into the water, let it stand for 24 hours. Then boil down to 2-1/2 quarts, and strain the liquid while hot. Add the sugar, and boil gradually for 1 hour. When cool, put into bottles or a jug, and keep corked.

In the Old West it was thought of as a valuable medicine to purify the blood, and used to help cases of general infirmity or weakness from any cause whatever.

Albuquerque 350 mi.

Phoenix 180 mi.
Denver 420 mi.

Salt Lake City 580 miles

Next Outpost:
2 days ride

It was also taken for liver ailments, dyspepsia, or indigestion, scrofula, female weakness, loss of appetite, effects of syphilis or venereal disease, and in every case where the wish was to build up and strengthen the system.

However, it was only used about 2 months at a time.

HOUSEHOLD HINTS

There are many pieces of conventional frontier wisdom that seem utterly useless today. In the Old West, this knowledge could make all the difference in how and at what comfort level you lived your life.

To purify muddy waters of rivers or pits: Make a number of holes in the bottom of a deep tub; lay some clean gravel thereon, and above this some clean sand; sink this tub in the river or pit, so that only a few inches of the tub will be above the surface of the water; the river or pit water will filter through the sand, and rise clear through it to the level of the water on the outside, and will be pure and limpid.

Easy way to mend cracks in stoves, pipes, or ovens: When a crack is discovered in a stove, through which the fire or smoke penetrates, the aperture may be completely closed in a moment with a composition consisting of wood ashes and common salt, made up into a paste with a little water, and plastered over the crack. This method is equally effective, whether the stove be cold or hot.

Eternal fence posts: Many years ago wood could be made to last longer than iron in the ground. The process is so simple and inexpensive. Use poplar, basswood, or quaking ash as any other kind of timber for fence posts. Posts taken out after having been set for ten years were known to be as sound as when they were first put into the ground. The posts can be prepared for less than two cents a piece.

This is how to do it: Take boiled linseed oil and stir in pulverized charcoal to the consistency of paint. Put a coat of this over the timber, and there is not a man who will live to see it rot.

To waterproof shoes: This simple and effectual remedy is nothing more than a little beeswax and mutton suet, warmed in a pipkin until a liquid state. Then rub some of it lightly over the edges of the soles where the stitches are, which will repel the wet, and not in the least prevent the blacking from having the usual effect.

Bed bug poison: Scotch snuff mixed with soft soap.

To prevent the smoking of a lamp: Soak the wick in strong vinegar, and dry it well before you use it. It will then burn both sweet and pleasant, and give much satisfaction for the trifling trouble.

To keep moths and beetles out of clothes: Put a piece of camphor in a linen bag, or some aromatic herbs, in the drawers, among linen or woolen clothes, and neither moth nor worm will come near them.

To make solid candles from common lard: Dissolve 1/4 pound of alum and 1/4 pound of saltpetre in 1/2 pint of water on a slow fire; then take 3 pounds of lard, cut into small pieces and put into the pot with this solution, stirring it constantly over a very moderate fire until the lard is dissolved; then let it simmer until all steam ceases to rise, and remove it from the fire at once. If you leave it too long it will get discolored. These candles are harder than ones made from tallow.

To revive old apple trees: Take fresh made lime from the kiln; slake it well with water, and well dress the tree with a brush, and the insects and moss will be completely destroyed. The outer ring will fall off, and a new smooth, clean, healthy one formed, and the tree assumes a most healthy appearance, and produce the finest fruit.

To remove paint from clothing: Use equal parts of ammonia and turpentine, well diluted with water. Wet the spot 2 or 3 times with the solution, then wash thoroughly with soapsuds.

SOAP

Pioneer wives had to first make their lye, before making soap. To make lye, place a barrel onto a frame high enough to put a good sized earthen vessel under it, for catching the lye. Bore a hole in the bottom of the barrel; place the earthen vessel under the hole. Put straw in the bottom of the barrel. Add 10 bushels of ashes for each bushel of unslacked lime. Ashes must be kept dry and they should be strong—hickory ashes are best.

Pour into the barrel one layer of ashes and on top of that place a layer of lime and add rainwater. Alternate the layers of ashes and lime until all are used up.

The lye will be ready as soon as it is strong enough to hold up an egg, and allow an area on top of the egg the size of a dime to be seen. When lye is not strong enough with the first run through, keep pouring it back through, and try adding a small amount of water.

TEN MINUTE LYE SOAP USING GREASE

two quarts of melted and strained grease
1-1/2 cupfuls of lye
l quart of water
1 cupful of household ammonia
2 tablespoonfuls of powdered borax
1/2 cup of warm water

Dissolve lye in 1 quart of water. Grease must be luke-warm; put grease into iron, enamel or granite pot (never in aluminum) and stir in lye.

Dissolve Borax in 1/2 cup of warm water. Add the ammonia and borax and stir all for 5 minutes by the clock. When hardened somewhat, cut into bars.

CAUTION: Stir the lye into the grease, NOT the grease into the lye.

LYE SOAP USING CRACKLINGS

one gallon of cracklings
1-1/2 cups of lye
2 quarts of water

Mix in soap kettle, or use enamel or granite pans. Mix well and boil 15 minutes, or until cracklings are well dissolved. Remove from fire and stir until it thickens. Pour into moulds and let harden and cut.

SEMINOLE HARD WHITE SOAP

Boil 15 pounds of lard or suet, and slowly add 6 gallons of liquid lye, strong enough to hold up an egg high enough to leave a piece as big as a quarter bare. Stir until thick, take out a little and cool, if no grease rises, it is done. If any grease appears, add more lye and boil up again. If it does not harden well on cooling, add some salt. If it is to be perfumed, melt it the next day, add the perfume, and run it in moulds or cut in cakes when cold. The best vessel for making this lye is the family cast iron boiling laundry pot.

RANCHER'S TOILET AND LAUNDRY SOAP

This soap was made by almost every ranchman's wife.

15 quarts of soft water
9 pounds of beef tallow or other grease
2 cans concentrated lye
1-1/2 pounds of rosin
1/2 pound Borax

Mix these ingredients together and boil about 3/4 hour, or longer if necessary. After it cools just a little, pour into a wooden box, cut into bars when set.
For toilet soap: Make the same way, but only use beef tallow. When it cools a little, add some peppermint oil for odor. You can beat it for a short time with an egg beater to make a lightweight toilet soap.

THE PIONEER KITCHEN

Like the camp cooks out on the trail, the housewife of the Old West spent a large part of her day preparing meals and cleaning up after meals, with much of the time in between taking care of other chores such as washing clothes and just general caretaking tasks. Any helpful hints that could make this work go a little easier were greatly valued and passed on to those who could use them. Here are a few pioneer shortcuts that have survived over the years.

To thin icing that is too thick, use a little milk. To thicken icing that is too thin, use a little powdered sugar.

To keep mashed potatoes warm for anyone late for dinner, place in top of a double boiler and place over hot water. Set on stove over low heat.

To keep pickles from molding, place a small piece of horseradish in jar on top of the pickles.

To make cake light and spongy add a tablespoon of warm water to the egg before mixing.

When cooking sauerkraut, add one teaspoon sugar.

For special touch with fried oysters serve with finely shredded cabbage salted with celery salt. It is very good.

When going camping take along a few cans of cream style corn. Fry bacon crisp in a Dutch oven or heavy frying pan, then pour out all but a little of the bacon grease. Pour in corn. After cooking for a short time, break 3 eggs into the corn and scramble. This makes a good breakfast along with the crisp, brown, and tender bacon.

When frying potatoes make them 1/3 carrots for a change. Then sprinkle a little flour over the potatoes and carrots.

To tenderize an old hen or prairie chicken cut up into serving pieces and slice the breast of the chicken. Soak in a little soda water all night, rinse well in cold water, then fry very slowly with a lid over the frying pan so as to steam the chicken.

For a lamb roast, brown well on top of stove, then stick 6 cloves into the roast and roast very slowly until tender. The taste will be more like deer meat than lamb.

For noodle soup, use good brown gravy left from a beef roast to make soup. Cook noodles in salt water. When tender, pour the gravy into the water and the noodles. Add black pepper to taste.

For an extended camping trip take along a yellow rain slicker so you can take a footbath like an old-time cowpuncher on a roundup. Just dig a small hole in the earth about the size of a wash basin, place slicker in the hole, pour in warm water. Sit down and stick your feet in the water.

For variations of fried mush boil a pot of yellow corn meal mush, making it thick. Dip a pan into ice-cold water then pour the mush into the pan. Let sit in a cold place to chill. Then slice, roll in corn meal, and fry until brown.

To whip thin cream dissolve 1 tablespoon of unflavored gelatin in 1 tablespoon of hot water. Then add to 2 cups of cream; chill for a few minutes, then whip.

To remove lime boil a cup of vinegar and a cup of water in a lime-coated teakettle. This will soften the sediment and it can easily be scraped off.

To tenderize meat add a tablespoon of vinegar to the water in which meats are boiled.

To brown fresh potatoes sprinkle a little flour over the pan of freshly sliced potatoes along with the pepper and salt. This will help to brown the fresh potatoes.

To peel oranges pour boiling water over oranges and let stand 5 minutes. This will cause the white lining to come away with the peeling when the oranges are to be sliced.

To scale fish more easily first dip fish into boiling water, then scale in usual manner.

To preserve eggs an old-time patented liquid is made like this: Take a bushel of lime, 2 pounds of salt, 1/2 pound of cream of tartar, and water enough to form a solution strong enough to float an egg. This liquid supposedly preserves eggs for 2 years.

SPANISH OLIVES

As the settlers moved westward during the Frontier period, they brought with them fixed ideas of their earlier customs of dress, social and economic life, and methods of food preparation. They adjusted these customs quickly to meet to the needs of their new environment, drawing from Indian, Mexican and Spanish cultures along the way. Early immigrants to California were discovered a highly civilized Spanish culture and such delicacies as the following--in use by the Spaniards since 1769!

Gather about 4 gallons of olives. Wash and clean thoroughly then place in an oak or crockery container. A vinegar barrel or 8 to 10 gallon stone jar is excellent. Cover with enough water so they can be stirred or agitated with a wooden paddle.

Pour 1 gallon of concentrated lye in the container and macerate for about 48 hours depending on the maturity of olives. Stir several times daily to permit lye to work evenly. Test several times by slitting fruit with knife to determine the action of the lye.

Very ripe olives must be processed carefully to prevent crushing, or breaking the skins. Very green olives can be cured, but will need a stronger solution, or a longer time for maceration, to soften and loosen from the seeds.

After curing, wash olives thoroughly and soak in fresh water for 2 or 3 days, or longer to eliminate lye. Change water occasionally, until it tastes fresh, or is neutral to litmus.

To start brine: Dump in 1 pound of salt. Add salt daily until suitable brine is formed. This is not stable, and should be renewed occasionally. Olives will keep much longer in a very heavy brine.

WARNING: Do Not Seal! These olives should be kept in an open container. Like all unpasteurized fruits and vegetables, if sealed they may develop the anaerobic Botulism bacillus, which is a dangerous organism. An open container will prevent this deadly risk.

Capture the Flavor of the Old West

Meals cooked on the trail or in a cozy pioneer kitchen had flavors and ingredients in common. We've take a look back at the cooks and foods of the Old West to give you a taste of the life and times as well as many authentic recipes that have been handed down from that period.

Also included are dishes that have been updated to reflect modern cooking methods and ingredients.

Enjoy your excursio into cooking in the Chuckwagon, Pione and Southwest trad tions as you recreat the flavors that wo the Old West.

ISBN 9781938653124

52995 >

9 781938 653124

CPSIA information can be obtained
at www.ICGtesting.com
Printed in the USA
LVHW09s2323100918
589410LV00003B/50/P